A Guide to Ethics and Moral Philosophy

A Guide to Ethics and Moral Philosophy

Brent Adkins

EDINBURGH
University Press

Edinburgh University Press is one of the leading university presses in the UK. We publish academic books and journals in our selected subject areas across the humanities and social sciences, combining cutting-edge scholarship with high editorial and production values to produce academic works of lasting importance. For more information visit our website: edinburghuniversitypress.com

Edinburgh University Press Ltd
The Tun – Holyrood Road, 12(2f) Jackson's Entry, Edinburgh EH8 8PJ

Typeset in 10/13 Gill Sans Nova by
IDSUK (DataConnection) Ltd, and
printed and bound in Great Britain by
CPI Group (UK) Ltd, Croydon CR0 4YY

A CIP record for this book is available from the British Library

ISBN 978 1 4744 2277 2 (hardback)
ISBN 978 1 4744 2279 6 (webready PDF)
ISBN 978 1 4744 2278 9 (paperback)
ISBN 978 1 4744 2280 2 (epub)

Contents

PART I ETHICS
HOW SHOULD WE LIVE?
ARISTOTLE AND SPINOZA

PART II MORALITY
HOW SHOULD WE ACT?
KANT AND MILL

PART III BEYOND
HOW MIGHT WE LIVE?
NIETZSCHE AND LEVINAS

Acknowledgments

I am very fortunate to work at Roanoke College, a college that encourages the exploration of the kind of fundamental questions found in this book. Working in such an environment has required me to continually refine my arguments and explanations in order to engage the students where they are. One student in particular, Hannah Schneider, has been of great help in this project, and I am grateful to her. I am also grateful for numerous colleagues across campus that have helped me think about this material in different contexts. The college itself supported this project through a sabbatical leave in the Fall of 2015. It is, indeed, a most excellent place to work. I would also like to thank Carol Macdonald at Edinburgh University Press for her usual aplomb in shepherding this project through the review and publication process, as well as the two anonymous reviewers that made helpful suggestions for the manuscript. Last, but not least, I would like to thank my family for their continuous and unwavering support.

Brent Adkins
July 2016

Glossary

Affect (*Spinoza*) – Any interaction of modes.

Appropriation (*Levinas*) – Making the other the same. Taking owner-ship of something that is not mine.

Asymmetry (*Levinas*) – In the ethical relation obligation only flows to the other. Ethics does not presuppose reciprocity.

Autonomy (*Kant*) – Self-ruling.

Bad conscience (*Nietzsche*) – Turning our dominating instincts inward instead of outward.

Bondage (*Spinoza*) – Being determined by causes opposed to one's nature.

Categorical imperative (*Kant*) – Laws that are their own end (X, because X is right).

Contingent (*Aristotle and Spinoza*) – What *can* be otherwise.

Debt (*Nietzsche*) – An economic relation whereby something is owed.

Duty (*Kant*) – What one *ought* to do. The path to goodness.

Emotion (*Spinoza*) – Affects that most concern human behavior. Love, hate, etc.

Ethics (*Levinas*) – A non-appropriating relation to the other.

Face (*Levinas*) – The literal face of the other person. That which calls us to justify our existence.

Freedom (*Spinoza*) – Understanding oneself, things, and the universe.

Genealogy (*Nietzsche*) – Nietzsche's method. It seeks the origin and value of philosophical terms.

General law (*Mill*) – Statistical likelihood. What is the case for most of the people most of the time.

Good (*Aristotle*) – What everything aims at.

Good (*Kant*) – Good will.

Good will (*Kant*) – The intentions behind an action.

Guilt (*Nietzsche*) – A psychological/theological relation whereby non-economic debt is incurred.

Habit (*Aristotle*) – Shaping character through conscious repetition.

Happiness (*Aristotle*) – An activity of the soul in accordance with virtue.

Happiness (*Mill*) – The concrete aggregate of things one cannot live without.

Heteronomy (*Kant*) – Being ruled by others.

Highest good (*Aristotle*) – The final aim. What all other goods point to.

Hypothetical imperative (*Kant*) – Laws that seek an end outside themselves (if X, then Y).

Inclination (*Kant*) – What one *wants* to do. The path to happiness.

Intellectual virtue (*Aristotle*) – A way of telling the truth.

Intention (*Kant*) – The reason or principle according to which one acts.

Intentionality (*Levinas*) – The appropriating relation between consciousness and its object.

Intuition (*Spinoza*) – Understanding that whatever is the case could not have been otherwise.

Justice (*Mill*) – The pursuits most likely to secure happiness. Justice is not opposed to happiness but part of it.

Justification (*Levinas*) – The problem of existence. How can we justify ourselves if others are suffering?

Knowledge (*Levinas*) – The appropriating relation between knower and known.

Maxim (*Kant*) – A rule for action.

Mode (*Spinoza*) – The parts of the whole. Humans are all modes.

Moral virtue (*Aristotle*) – Acting reasonably with regard to actions and emotions.

Morality (*Nietzsche*) – Our current value system. It is organized around the opposition between "good" and "evil."

Necessary (*Aristotle and Spinoza*) – What *cannot* be otherwise.

Other (*Levinas*) – That which lies outside appropriation.

Philology (*Nietzsche*) – The historical study of languages.

Pleasure (*Mill*) – There are two basics types: high and low. High pleasures are pleasures of the mind. Low pleasures are pleasures of the body.

Power (*Nietzsche*) – The ability or capacity of anything to establish and expand its area of control.

Power (*Spinoza*) – Ability or capacity.

Principle of utility (*Mill*) – Actions are right to the degree that they produce the greatest happiness for the greatest number.

Reason (*Spinoza*) – Seeing the necessary interconnection of things.

Resentment (*Nietzsche*) – The hatred of the strong by the weak. Nietzsche uses the French "*ressentiment.*"

Right (*Mill*) – That which we are justified in demanding that others defend in us.

Sanction (*Mill*) – Authorization.

Soul (*Aristotle*) – The form of a living thing.

Substance (*Spinoza*) – That which everything is a part of. The whole. The universe. God.

Universal law (*Mill*) – Necessity. What is the case without exception.

Virtue (*Aristotle*) – Excellence. Acting in accord with reason.

Virtue (*Spinoza*) – Power.

Will (*Kant*) – The faculty that creates and follows laws/imperatives.

Wisdom (*Levinas*) – That which lies beyond traditional philosophy.

Timeline

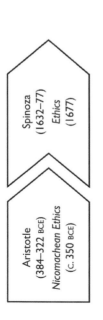

Aristotle
(384–322 BCE)
Nicomachean Ethics
(c. 350 BCE)

Spinoza
(1632–77)
Ethics
(1677)

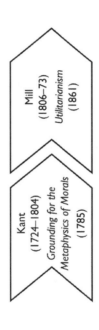

Kant
(1724–1804)
*Grounding for the
Metaphysics of Morals*
(1785)

Mill
(1806–73)
Utilitarianism
(1861)

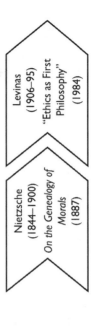

Nietzsche
(1844–1900)
*On the Genealogy of
Morals*
(1887)

Levinas
(1906–95)
"Ethics as First
Philosophy"
(1984)

Introduction: Three Questions

How should we live?

How should we act?

How might we live?

At first glance these questions seem really similar, but even though they differ from one another by one or two words only, it turns out that these small differences in the questions lead to vastly different answers. Two drops of rain landing on top of a mountain may wind up thousands of miles from one another, depending on what side they roll down. In the case of the three questions above, the answers hinge on the difference between living and acting and between should and might. In the case of living and acting the difference may not seem worth pursuing. After all, each term seems necessary for the other. I cannot act without living, and I cannot live without acting. This mutual dependence, however, does not mean that we cannot make a distinction in principle. This becomes clear when we think about different ways in which we use these words. Take the phrase "standard of living," for example. This phrase has all sorts of implications about annual income, housing, clothing, and entertainment built into it. It implies a baseline, a standard, by which we can gauge our lives as a whole, and it is really this notion of "wholeness" that interests us here. While the phrase "standard of acting" is not nearly as common as "standard of living," the implications are clearly different. A standard of acting usually concerns actions in specific situations, and does not suggest "wholeness" in the same way that standard of living does. Thus, the questions How should we live? and How should we act? require very different answers, because one is seeking a kind of summary claim about the best kind of life to live, while the other is asking for a judgment about the rightness or wrongness of individual acts.

The third question, How might we live?, returns to the connotations of wholeness found in the first question, but it replaces "should" with "might." "Should" suggests requirement and obligation. I am accountable for the things I should do and blameworthy if I fail to do them. "Might," in contrast, suggests openness and possibility. "Might" is not dependent on prescription, but seeks new ways of living. "Might" suggests an experimental form of life. "Might" also has a critical edge. In order to know how we might live, we also need to know how we have lived. Thus, figuring out what is possible for a life requires us to see the limits of other ways of living and acting. An experimental life also foregoes the certainties provided by "should." "Should" maps out everything in advance. From the perspective of "should" our life and actions either conform to predetermined categories or they do not. There is comfort in this kind of clarity, and this is why "should" has been so important for thinking about living and acting. Without the certainties provided by "should," "might" is a much riskier and much rarer undertaking.[1]

The primary aim of this book is to give you an opportunity to think through your own answers to these three questions. On the one hand, I am convinced that everyone already has intuitive answers to these questions. That is, everyone has a philosophy, and answers to these questions are components of it. On the other hand, precisely because the answers to these questions are formed so young and so deeply, we rarely take the opportunity to revisit our answers to these questions. This book provides such an opportunity in the hope that we might be able to answer these questions more clearly and consistently.

While there are numerous ways that we might examine our own philosophies, this book takes a historical approach. Philosophies are not developed in a vacuum but are part of a larger conversation about ways in which other people have answered these three basic questions. In this regard the book provides a narrative by which you can orient yourself as you begin to think about your own philosophy. Although everybody must answer these basic questions of philosophy, historically it has been the case that one of the questions has been dominant.

---

[1] The distinction between How should we live? and How should we act? is longstanding. I first came across the third question, How might we live?, in Todd May's *Gilles Deleuze: An Introduction*.

In the case of Western philosophy, How should we live? is the inaugural and longest-reigning of the questions. We will begin there with Aristotle's answer to the question in his justly famous treatise on the good life, the *Nicomachean Ethics*. Remarkably, despite being written 2,500 years ago, Aristotle vision of living well remains compelling. This speaks not only to Aristotle's genius but also to the enormous influence he had and continues to have on our thought.

After Aristotle, we will skip the intervening two millennia to the work of Spinoza. I do not mean to suggest that nothing happens between Aristotle and Spinoza, but I do want to use Spinoza as a foil to Aristotle. Even though Spinoza is answering the same question as Aristotle, his historical circumstances are very different. The principal differences that shape Spinoza's answer to the question How should we live? are Christianity and the dawn of the scientific revolution. It is no longer possible for Spinoza to avoid the conflict between science and religion, especially as both relate to the best kind of life to live. If science and religion give different answers at this point, what resources do we have to help us decide about what kind of life to lead? Spinoza is particularly challenging because he gives well-reasoned arguments for positions most people find disturbing.

Even though How should we live? served longest as the organizing question of philosophy, not long after Spinoza a new question displaces it. Beginning with Kant, the dominant question becomes How should we act? In many ways, Kant inherits Spinoza's concerns about religion and science but approaches them very differently because his philosophy is oriented toward a different question. Kant argues that the key to answering the question of right action lies in understanding and correcting the intentions behind the action. In contrast to this, Mill, Kant's near-contemporary, argues that right action simply cannot be determined by intentions. Only the consequences of action can determine whether the action is good. The debate between intentions and consequences still rages today, and we often shift indiscriminately between these two positions as we attempt to determine the rightness of our actions.

The final question, How might we live?, is the most recent and least explored. We will look at the philosophies of Nietzsche and Levinas as guided by this question. What Nietzsche and Levinas both have in common, though two world wars lie between their work, is the concern that something has gone wrong with the project of philosophy at its very core. Furthermore, both seek to go beyond the limits of philosophy as it has been traditionally defined. Despite these convergences, Nietzsche and Levinas differ radically and profoundly about the direction that philosophy might take. Nietzsche attempts to recast philosophy and life itself as a work of art, while Levinas argues that life can only be lived in an ethical relationship to another person.

Taken as a whole, then, the book seeks to provide both a timeline and a conceptual geography of philosophy. It first maps out the kingdom of "ethics," a realm organized around living well. Though the kingdom had many rulers, we will focus on two: Aristotle, one of the early founding kings, and Spinoza, a later king beset by threats from the kingdoms of science and religion. The kingdom of "ethics" is supplanted by the republic of "morality," where everyone is both a lawgiver and bound by the moral law. Kant and Mill are the chief architects of the republic. Both agree that the republic of morality is designed to answer the question How should we act?, but they are profoundly at odds about the best way to answer this question. Neither the kingdom of ethics nor the republic of morality has been without its detractors. This resistance coalesces in the late nineteenth and early twentieth centuries in the figures of Nietzsche and Levinas. They are not seeking to refound the kingdom of ethics or shore up the republic of morality. They are calling the very possibility of both into question. They are seeking something "beyond." Nietzsche and Levinas's question is How might we live?, but their answers are diametrically opposed.

So, as you travel through this country with its deep sedimentations, always bear in mind where and when you are. More importantly, always bear in mind *who* you are. Never stop asking yourself What do I think about this? Which of my presuppositions are being called into question? Could I live like this? That is the task of philosophy.

PART I ETHICS

HOW SHOULD WE LIVE?
ARISTOTLE AND SPINOZA

Ethics

The two philosophers that we will read about in this section are Aristotle and Spinoza. Aristotle (384–322 BCE) is one of the giants in the history of philosophy. He was a student of Plato and the teacher of Alexander the Great. His works are remarkable for the breadth of material that they cover. He wrote works of biology, logic, theology, psychology, politics, ethics, and many others. All of these were part of philosophy for Aristotle.

Two thousand years separates the work of Aristotle and the work of Benedict de Spinoza (1632–77 CE), and much changes in the intervening millennia. Chief among these changes is the dominance of Christianity in Europe. Spinoza is writing during a time that is beginning to question this dominance, especially with regard to mathematics and science. Spinoza is one of the main champions of the "new learning" that eventually revolutionizes thought in what we commonly call the Enlightenment. Though Spinoza does not write as much as Aristotle, his works are equally comprehensive.

Despite the vast gulf of history that separates Aristotle and Spinoza, both are answering the same question, How should we live? This is the question of ethics, *par excellence*. It is a question that pursues the nature of human life as a whole and the way to pursue this life as rationally as possible. As a result, both Aristotle and Spinoza will explore human nature and its proper place in the larger scheme of things in an attempt to articulate a life well lived.

They both think that reason is the key to living well, but they define reason differently. The task of this section is to clarify not only *what* Aristotle and Spinoza thought, but also *why* they thought the way they did. Once we see the reasons behind their positions, we can begin to form our own arguments about the best kind of life to live.

1

Aristotle: Happiness is the Good
(*Nicomachean Ethics*, Books 1 and 2)

Key terms

Good – What everything aims at.
Highest good – The final aim. What all other goods point to.
Happiness – An activity of the soul in accordance with virtue.
Soul – The form of a living thing.
Virtue – Excellence. Acting in accord with reason.

One of the primary tasks of philosophy has to be defining what "good" is. I cannot very well pursue the good life or even right action, unless I know what "good" is. This is precisely where Aristotle begins his *Nicomachean Ethics*. He writes, "the good, therefore, has been well defined as that at which all things aim" (EN I.1, 1094a3).[1]

The first thing to note about this definition is that Aristotle does not claim it as his own. He simply notes that other people have looked into this problem of the good already, and some sort of consensus has been reached. Often Aristotle will take received wisdom such as this and argue that it is mistaken in some fundamental way. In this

---

[1] In order to make my citations as easy as possible to find, I provide two sets of references in Aristotle. The first reference (e.g., "EN I.1") indicates the book number followed by the chapter number. In this case, the reference is to Book One, Chapter One. The second reference (e.g., "1094a3") refers to marginal numbers that are found in most editions of Aristotle's works. These numbers give both a location in the text, 1094a, and a line number, 3. The edition I'm using here is Aristotle, *Nicomachean Ethics*, trans. Martin Ostwald (Englewood Cliffs, NJ: Prentice Hall, 1962). The citations will work for any edition of the *Ethics*.

case, however, Aristotle proceeds as if he is in agreement with the definition.

Two immediate problems arise with this definition, though. The first problem concerns the broadness of the definition. How does knowing that all actions aim at the good actually help us? It looks as if, if all actions aim at the good, then it would be impossible to *not* aim at the good. But does the very worth of philosophy not depend on distinguishing the good life from lives less well lived? How is this kind of distinction possible if *all actions* aim at the good? The short response to this objection is that there is a difference between aiming at a target and hitting it. One of the tasks of the *Nicomachean Ethics* is not simply to record what we are aiming at, but also to explain to us how to actually hit it.

The second (and more serious) problem with the definition of the good as that at which all things aim is that it seems obviously false. Surely, people aim at bad things all the time. Does a bank robber aim at the good? I think everyone would agree that there is something off about the kind of life that the bank robber has chosen. Yet suppose we change the question slightly to Does the bank robber aim at *a* good? Here our answer shifts uncomfortably into the affirmative. Yes, the bank robber aims at a good: namely, money. So, now the definition of good is not obviously false. It does seem that whatever horrible action we might name, there is some good being pursued there, even if it is not *the* good.

Aristotle draws two conclusions from this result. First, there are many kinds of goods, and these goods are organized hierarchically. Thus, while everyone can agree that money is a good, there are higher goods that might prevent one from pursuing money by any means necessary. Second, it is possible that people can be confused about where a particular good stands in relation to other goods: say, the good of having money in relation to the good of staying out of jail. It is also possible that people can be confused about the best way to achieve a particular good. Thus, the bank robber is doubly confused, not only about where money stands in relation to other goods, but also about the best way to acquire money. The *Nicomachean Ethics* seeks to alleviate confusions such as these by arguing that there is a highest good around which all other goods are organized and by demonstrating the best way to achieve the highest good (EN I.1, 1094a5–18).

The highest good is happiness

Aristotle seems to be on solid ground when he claims that some goods are superior to other goods. This is easily demonstrated with regard to money. Unless one is a coin collector, no one wants money for the sake of money, not even the bank robber. People want money so that they can buy things with it: houses, cars, food, etc. Thus, these other goods, the ones people will trade money for, are superior to money itself. It is not clear at all, though, how the fact that some goods are superior to others leads to the supposition of a highest good. Sure, lots of things are better than money, but are houses better than cars? And what is better than both of those? How would one go about proving something like that? In order to answer these questions, let's try a little thought experiment. It takes the form of a conversation that I have with almost all of my classes:

Me: Why are you here?
Student: This class is required for a degree.
Me: Why do you want a degree?
Student: A degree will help me get a job.
Me: Why do you want a job?
Student: So I can make money.
Me: Why do you want money?
Student: So I can buy things.
Me: Why do you want those things?
Student: Those things will make me happy.
Me: Why do you want to be happy?
Student: Uh, I don't know, because being happy is better than not being happy.

To begin with, I have had this (nearly) exact conversation dozens of times in dozens of classes over the last twenty years or so. I am highly confident that the results would be the same in any situation. I could stop random people in the street or in a coffee shop and ask, "Why are you here?" Assuming they would answer me, and even though the path will differ, if I keep asking "Why" long enough, I will eventually get the answer, "Because it will make me happy." If I press beyond that to ask, "Why do you want to be happy?", I get looks of incredulity and non-answers that simply restate the desire to be happy. For Aristotle, the fact that asking "why" about any given action, getting coffee or sitting in class, ultimately (always) leads to a claim about happiness suggests, at the very least, that happiness must rank very high on the scale of goods. Furthermore, the fact that there does not seem to be anything beyond happiness for which we want to be happy suggests that happiness is itself a very good candidate for the highest good. Thus, statements such as "I do X, because it makes me happy" are perfectly plausible, and the X can be replaced with any number of things. If we reverse the statement, though, and make happiness the means rather than the end, "I pursue happiness, so that I can do X," then it becomes very difficult to imagine what X might be. Aristotle thus concludes that not only does everyone want to be happy, but also that everything everyone does is an attempt (either directly or indirectly) to achieve happiness (EN I.5, 1095b15–1096a10; EN I.7, 1097b1–6).

Happiness is flourishing

Supposing that we grant Aristotle's conclusion that all things aim at some good and that the highest good is happiness, this still leaves a huge question unanswered. What is happiness? Most people today use the word "happiness" as synonymous with "pleasure." We can see this usage clearly in the phrase, "that makes me happy." People who say this do not think that anything like the highest good has been achieved. All they mean is that the particular object or event they are referring to gives them pleasure. "This ice cream makes me so happy." "I'm so happy to hear that we're in the same class." Other philosophers we will read about later, such as Kant and Mill, agree with our everyday usage and equate happiness and pleasure. Aristotle, however, does not think that happiness and pleasure are the same thing. In fact, just to be clear, we can turn this into a sort of equation that we can return to later to compare these philosophers with one another. For Aristotle:

Happiness ≠ Pleasure

The difference between happiness and pleasure is going to cause two problems, one for us, one for Aristotle. The problem for Aristotle is that he still needs to explain how pleasure fits into the well-lived life, even if it is not the highest good. We will look at his arguments concerning the role of pleasure in the next chapter. The problem for us will be reminding ourselves that whenever Aristotle uses the word "happiness" he does not mean "pleasure." This will take some getting used to. In order to facilitate this transition, I propose (along with a lot of other people writing about Aristotle) to replace the word "happiness" with the word "flourishing." The reason for this switch (beyond avoiding confusion) lies in Aristotle's works beyond the *Nicomachean Ethics* (EN I.4, 1095a20–2).

Aristotle wrote on almost every conceivable topic: biology, art, politics, psychology, logic, physics, theology, and metaphysics. Several constants run through all of these works and show Aristotle to be a formidable thinker. Chief among these constants is Aristotle's curiosity about the world. This curiosity is always driving his attempt to make sense of the world as fundamentally orderly. As a result, he is a systematic thinker who tries to organize knowledge into schemes of increasing generality. So, for example, biology, "the study of living things," is important in its own right, but how does it relate to physics? Is it a subset of physics with overlapping principles? Or, are they distinct realms of inquiry? How do both of these relate to human psychology? How do all three of these relate to politics? How do all of these relate to the question of the highest good? In order to answer these questions, Aristotle uses one of his most enduring contributions to the world: logic. Aristotle does not simply state his position. He gives us the reasons that led him to that position, and the reasons why he rejected the other competing positions. One of the most important tasks in philosophy is to follow Aristotle's lead here. You are not required to agree with Aristotle, but it is imperative that you give reasons for your position. This is the mark of good philosophy.

The metaphysics and psychology of flourishing

In order to understand Aristotle's concern with human flourishing more fully, let's take a brief look at some of those other works: namely, his *Metaphysics* and his psychology (from the work *On the Soul*, sometimes called *De Anima*, which is Latin for "on the soul"). Aristotle did not name his work "*Metaphysics*." It was simply the work that came after his book on physics, but the name stuck and 2,500 years later we still call the kinds of things Aristotle was talking about in that book "metaphysics." What exactly was Aristotle talking about, though? He was trying to think through the most basic nature of reality, what is really real. We typically think of the real in material terms. What is real is what we can see and touch. However, we also typically think that minds and thoughts are also real, even if we cannot see and touch them. In this respect, most of us have a "dualist" metaphysics. That is, we think two very different kinds of things are real. Aristotle sees the same problem, but he solves it differently. For our purposes here, I would like to look at the two elements that Aristotle thought composed all things. The first element is "matter." Aristotle thought that there must be some "stuff" out of which everything is made. However, we never see stuff or matter by itself. The stuff always has a definitive shape. This shape or form that stuff takes is the second element. Everything has both a form and a matter, a shape and a stuff. Thus, a table is material that has been given the form of a table. A computer is material that has been given the form of a computer. Even though we do not normally separate out these two elements, Aristotle's metaphysical claim is that these two elements are what is really there.[2]

There is more to the story, though. While Aristotle thinks that stuff or matter is pretty much the same everywhere and in everything, there seems to be some pretty important differences among the shapes of things. It is astoundingly important to me that my computer has a different shape from my desk. It is also important that my phone has a different shape from a cup of tea. How should we characterize these differences in shape? Obviously, we could characterize them in all sorts of ways – height, weight, density, etc. – but it is not clear that would get at what is really important here. What's really important is that the shape of something determines what it is capable of. The relevant difference in shape between my desk and my computer boils down to the fact that my desk holds up my computer very nicely but only my computer can store what I type on it with a keyboard. No amount of tapping in any order will allow my desk to store retrievable documents. We can summarize this difference in shape between the

---

[2] Aristotle, *Metaphysics* Z.3, 1029a1–5. The same principles apply for citing the *Metaphysics*. Here Z = Zeta = Book 7.

desk and computer in one word, "complexity." The complexity of the computer's shape is what allows it to do things that the desk cannot. Furthermore, notice here the relation among shape, complexity, and function. The form determines the function, and as the complexity of the form increases, so does the complexity of the function (EN I.7, 1098a7–16).

For Aristotle, while we can easily rank things according to their complexity, there is one point at which the complexity takes such a qualitative leap that it warrants special consideration. That leap occurs in the shift from inanimate to animate objects, from the non-living to the living. While technological complexity is increasing at a staggering rate, Aristotle would think that even that pales in comparison to a tree's ability to grow from a tiny seed. Aristotle was so struck by this difference between living and non-living things that he reserved a special word for the shape of living things. He called the form of a living thing "soul." This will be a recurring theme throughout the book, but clearly Aristotle is using the word "soul" differently from the way we use it. We tend to use the word "soul" with Platonic and Christian connotations to mean something like "our innermost and (usually) immortal self." All Aristotle means by it, though, is "the shape of a living organism."[3]

Of course, even souls can be distinguished by their complexity. For Aristotle, humans are more complex than animals, and animals are more complex than plants. How can we characterize these differences, though? Well, if the complexity of function increases with the complexity of form, we should be able to distinguish among these forms according to their function. So, what does a plant do that non-living things cannot do? Although we might have hard questions for Aristotle about things like crystals, plants can grow and absorb nutrients. What can animals do that plants cannot? Animals can move, and they are motivated to move by pursuing pleasure and avoiding pain. Striking a plant will not cause it to run away in pain. Notice that Aristotle's argument here concerns the function or capabilities that set(s) plants or animals apart. He is not claiming that animals do not grow and take in nutrients. He is only claiming that what is important, what is defining for animals, their specific difference, is their movement and motivation.

---

[3] *De Anima* II.1, 412a20.

This is an added complexity, not a complexity that eliminates lower forms of complexity.[4]

Humans obviously grow and take in nutrients. They also obviously move and are motivated by pleasure and pain, but Aristotle does not want to know what humans have in common with plants and animals. He wants to know what sets them apart. What can humans do that plants and animals cannot? They can reason. As we will see in the next chapter, reason itself is complex and has many facets. For right now, though, let's focus on the implications of the differences in complexity among these different types of living things (EN I.13, 1102a5–1102b5).[5] Here is a picture that summarizes Aristotle's claims about the soul up to this point:

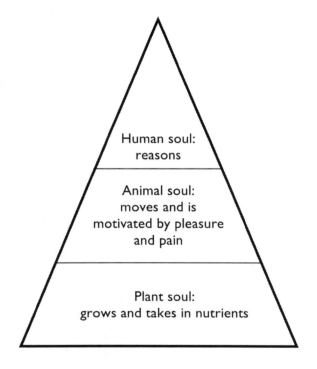

Human soul:
reasons

Animal soul:
moves and is
motivated by pleasure
and pain

Plant soul:
grows and takes in nutrients

[4] *Metaphysics* Z.12, 1037b9–1038a10.
[5] *De Anima* II.3, 414a25–425a15.

Now that we have the basics concerning Aristotle's conception of the soul, we can return to why "flourishing" is a better way to talk about the good life than "happiness." It would seem strange to talk about the "happiness" of plants, but it makes perfect sense to talk about a plant "flourishing." How do we know when a plant is flourishing? When it is green. When it is blooming. When it is growing. Notice that all of the signs of flourishing are related to the plant's soul. We know a plant is flourishing when it is growing and taking in nutrients. A plant is flourishing when it is doing what sets it apart from inanimate objects. We can say the same thing about animals. An animal is flourishing when it moves to keep itself healthy in accordance with pleasure and pain. In contrast, we would never say an animal that simply grows and takes in nutrients, but never moves, is flourishing.[6]

Aristotle makes the same case for humans. We would never say that a human who simply takes in nutrients or simply follows pleasure and pain is flourishing. There is more to human life than there is to plant or animal life. This more is reflected in our shape, our souls, our capacity for reason. Human flourishing must be related to what sets us apart, not to what we have in common with other living things. Also, there is an important distinction between possessing the capacity to reason and acting on it. For Aristotle, all humans possess the capacity for reason, but humans only flourish to the degree that they act in accord with this capacity. While I possess the capacity to play basketball, I am not a basketball player unless I actually play. Thus, happiness or human flourishing is not an emotion or state of being or even a capacity. It is an activity. Happiness is acting according to the best part of who we are. Human flourishing is acting according to reason. The remainder of the *Nicomachean Ethics* is primarily concerned with how we act according to reason (EN II.4, 1105a30–5).

Acting according to reason is virtue

The word that Aristotle uses to name "acting according to reason" is "virtue." Since "virtue" today has almost exclusively moral connotations, and since we rarely use the word any more, it might be helpful to also use the word "excellence." For Aristotle, acting according to

---

[6] Ibid.

reason is acting excellently or virtuously. We can get a sense of what he has in mind if we think of the experience commonly referred to as being "in the zone." This is often used in the context of competitive sports, but it happens in all areas of life. It refers to when, after long years of practice and honing your skills, there are those rare occasions you find yourself on the court and can do no wrong. Everyone else seems to be moving in slow motion. You do not feel your feet touch the floor. Your energy is limitless and everything you do works. All your shots hit their mark. When everything clicks like this, you are flourishing as a player, and your flourishing is nothing other than your excellent activity. It takes a lot of hard work to get to this point. It never happens by accident. Aristotle is arguing that excellent activity like this is the key to a life well lived. The question is How can we expand this activity beyond fleeting moments in a game to our whole lives (EN I.7, 1098a15)?

The answer to this question lies (not surprisingly) in the deployment of reason. For Aristotle, the human soul is a battleground between its rational and irrational parts. The more we can extend the rule of reason, the happier we will be. Using the distinctions we made above concerning the different parts of the soul, let's think about which parts are rational, which are irrational, and which could be susceptible to reason. The rational part is clearly the human soul. Reason is its defining characteristic. The irrational part is the plant soul. No matter how much I think and deliberate about it, I cannot reason with that part of me that grows and takes in nutrients. I cannot begin to metabolize rocks simply because I'm hungry now and it would be convenient to do so. I cannot reason with my pituitary gland to grow another four inches, so that I can become a more excellent basketball player. The plant soul is immune to reason and thus remains fundamentally irrational. What about the animal soul, though? Here it looks as if there might be a role for reason. While my movements on a basketball court are not naturally excellent, I can see that with some (OK, lots and lots of) training they could be made so (EN I.13, 1102a25–1102b10).

Kinds of virtue or excellence

Using reason to guide one's actions is not the only purpose that reason serves with regard to our animal souls. It is also the case that reason can guide our responses to pleasure and pain. Think of all the things that we do or do not do out of fear of pain or hope for pleasure. Imagine a small child who is afraid to jump into a swimming pool. We coax and cajole the child, show her that there is nothing to be afraid of. Eventually, she overcomes her fear and jumps into the pool. We praise her for this small bit of courage in the hope that she will continue to face and overcome her fears and thus excel. For us, having gained some mastery over fear, it is easy to see that a life lived courageously is happier than a life lived in fear. We do not say that someone living in constant fear is flourishing. Our animal souls are this complex locus of action and emotion rooted in responses to pleasure and pain. To the degree that we can guide these responses to pleasure and pain by reason, we flourish.

Aristotle calls the control of the animal soul by reason "moral virtue." If we recall that "soul" for Aristotle means "form" or "shape," we can say that the animal soul is malleable, subject to forces of reason and unreason. When we use reason to shape our animal souls, we flourish. A lot of this shaping of our animal souls occurs in childhood. We imitate our parents, siblings, and friends. This imitation shapes us. We also receive direct instruction from parents and teachers about how to act. This instruction also shapes us. "For moral excellence is concerned with pleasure and pain ... for this reason Plato says, men must be brought up from childhood to feel pleasure and pain at the proper things; for this is correct education" (1104b9–13).

There is more to virtue than responding to pleasure and pain, though. Beyond acting excellently there is also thinking excellently. Even though all humans have the capacity for reason, it does not follow that all humans use it well or even at all. Aristotle calls excellent thinking "intellectual virtue." As it turns out, the reasonable part of our souls is also malleable. The shape that we give it determines whether we think well or poorly. As we will see, though, excellent use of reason does not work the same way as the moral virtues. At the same time, Aristotle is convinced that human flourishing is just as dependent on thinking excellently as it is on acting excellently (EN I.13, 1103a5–10).

For Aristotle the goal of human life is happiness, but happiness is not pleasure or a fleeting feeling of any kind. It is an activity, "an activity of the soul in conformity with virtue" (1099b26). Furthermore, this virtue is complex in exactly the same way that the soul is complex. Just as there are different parts of the soul, there are different kinds of virtue corresponding to these different parts. The plant soul is not amenable to reason, so there are no virtues attached to it. The animal soul, however, is amenable to reason. Insofar as reason governs the animal soul, we call that "moral virtue." We call the way in which reason governs the intellect, though, "intellectual virtue."

The virtues, taken as whole, concern human life as a whole. Aristotle's philosophy examines the whole person in the context of a whole life. Though he admits that it is very difficult to live well, it is nonetheless a task worth pursuing. It is worth pursuing because a life well lived is its own reward. Furthermore, since such a life arises out of the way we shape ourselves through reason, the happiness found here is not easily lost. So, for those willing to undergo the hard work of shaping themselves according to reason, Aristotle is ready to be your guide. In the next chapter we will look at how both the moral and intellectual virtues are acquired, the tricky role of pleasure, and possibility of the highest happiness (EN I.10, 1100b12–21).

Summary

For Aristotle, happiness/flourishing is not an emotion but an activity. We are only flourishing when we act according to the best part of who we are, when we act according to reason. Human flourishing requires much effort and a good education.

Questions

1. Is happiness/flourishing the highest good?
2. Is reason necessary for human flourishing?
3. Can you give examples of people you think are flourishing?
   Why did you choose them?
   Do you think Aristotle would agree?

2

Aristotle: Virtue and the Highest Happiness
(*Nicomachean Ethics*, Books 2, 6 and 10)

Key terms

Habit – Shaping character through conscious repetition.
Moral virtue – Acting reasonably with regard to actions and emotions.
Intellectual virtue – A way of telling the truth.
Necessary – What *cannot* be otherwise.
Contingent – What *can* be otherwise.

In the previous chapter we saw that Aristotle makes the argument that we are happiest when we're doing things that we are good at. Based on that claim, Aristotle argues that there are two basic ways that we are good: good actions and good thinking. Ultimately, Aristotle thinks that thinking is a kind of action, but it is a qualitatively different kind of action from those that arise with respect to pleasure and pain. We could even go so far as to say that, for Aristotle, actions that arise from pleasure and pain are animal actions, and the task is to make them human actions by bringing them under the sway of reason. Doing these actions well is what Aristotle calls "moral virtue." Aristotle calls thinking well "intellectual virtue." In this chapter, we will look at Aristotle's arguments for acquiring both kinds of virtue, since flourishing simply is acting in accord with virtue.

Moral virtues are acquired by habit

Humans form habits. They have habits related to walking, talking, sitting, standing, eating, drinking, laughing, etc. Almost any action is intertwined with habit in some way. This is a good thing, too. Think how hard it would be to do the most basic tasks if we had to think about every single movement. I shudder to think how long it would take me to write anything, if I had not formed a habit with regard to my fingers and the keyboard. Aristotle recognizes that habits constitute a large part of our behavior. The question is not whether to form habits, but whether we will form good or bad habits. Good habits are the key to moral virtue for Aristotle. Acting on those good habits is flourishing.

Let's take a look at a simple habit that you probably formed without giving it much thought. Hold your hands as far apart as possible and clap them together so that your fingers interlace. If you are right-handed you will probably find that your left thumb is on top and your right pinky is on the bottom. Whatever order your fingers are in, the way you are doing it now feels comfortable, even "natural." Of course, it is not really "natural" in the sense that you were born doing it that way and could not change it if you wanted to, like your height or the length or your second toe. This feeling of "naturalness" in connection with habits is so pervasive that the term "second nature" was coined for it. The fact is that you can change the order in which your fingers interlace. It just takes a little practice. Try clapping your hands together again, but this time switch it up so that the opposite thumb is on top and the opposite pinky is on the bottom. The first thing you notice is that it is hard to do. Habits are hard to break. That is why Aristotle is so concerned that we learn to form good habits early on. The second thing you notice is that it feels weird and awkward to interlace your fingers in this way. It is unpleasant. This reminds us that actions are connected to pleasure and pain. However, if you really wanted to, you could break the habit of interlacing your fingers one way and replace it with the habit of interlacing your fingers the other way. How? Practice. Simply override your usual habit and consciously choose to do it the other way. Eventually, you will develop a new habit of interlacing your fingers and the old way will feel strange and uncomfortable (EN II.1, 1103a15–25).

Admittedly, not much is at stake in how we interlace our fingers. People are not (as far as I know) praised or blamed according to how they interlace their fingers. Even in actions where much is at stake, though, the process of habit formation is the same. Habits are acquired by practicing an action over and over again until it becomes fixed, second nature. Today we might be more likely to call it "muscle memory," but the necessity of repetition remains a constant. I become a good free throw shooter by shooting free throws over and over again. Or, more precisely, I become a good free throw shooter by shooting free throws well repeatedly. If I shoot free throws poorly over and over again, I will become a bad free throw shooter (EN II.1, 1103a25–35).

It is also really important to have someone who can show me how to do it right. Habits are best formed by imitation. For example, it is so much easier for me to learn how to play a song on guitar if I can watch someone else playing it. In that respect Youtube is a goldmine. There is such a huge difference between someone saying (or writing), "Play an A7sus2," and someone showing me where to put my fingers. Aristotle also recognizes the importance of being shown rather than told how to act. If you want to flourish, find someone who is already flourishing and imitate that person. By the same token, if you imitate people who are not flourishing, you will acquire their bad habits and fail to flourish yourself (EN II.1, 1103b6–25; EN II.6, 1107a1).

Moral Virtue is Found on a Mean

We develop habits through imitation and repetition, but the goal we are really after is good habits. That is where excellence lies. How do we find that? In order to answer this question we need to look at the intersection between excellence and action. For Aristotle, every action is some kind of exertion or effort. The amount of effort that we put forth lies somewhere on a continuum. The end points of the continuum are too much effort, an excess, and too little effort, a deficiency. We can illustrate this in a thousand ways. If I am shooting a basketball, is it possible to shoot too far? Is it possible not to shoot far enough? If I decide that I'd like to become a competitive body builder, is it possible to work out too little? Is it possible to work out too much? Is it possible to eat too little or too much?

We can easily see that the answer is "yes" to all of these questions. If we ask a further question, How much effort is the right amount of effort?, doesn't the answer have to be somewhere between too much and too little? Thus, the virtue or excellence of an action lies on a mean between excess and deficiency. Making a basket means putting exactly the right amount of effort into the shot. We can picture this simply:

Excess   Virtue   Deficiency

Let's take a concrete example to illustrate Aristotle's point here. Fear is a painful emotion that can spur all sorts of actions. The question is What is the excellent response to fear? How can we flourish with respect to our fear? As we saw above, excellence lies somewhere between excess and deficiency. What do we call actions that evidence too much fear? Cowardice. What do we call actions that evidence too little fear? Rashness. What is the right way to act with regard to our fear? What do we call the median between cowardice and rashness? Courage. Our picture from above now looks like this:

Cowardice   Courage   Rashness

At this point we can note two important things. First, every moral virtue has two related vices, corresponding to the excess and deficiency of a given action. Second, the excess and deficiency are of the action or emotion, not of the virtue. Rashness is not an excess of courage. Cowardice is not a deficiency of courage. Virtue does not have a mean. It is the mean. The mean is always the mean of a particular action or emotion. Thus, rashness is a deficiency of fear, and cowardice is an excess of fear (EN II.2, 1103b25–1104b1).

The mean is not mathematical

To say that virtue lies on a mean between two extremes does not quite tell us what we really need to know. It is obviously true, but true in the way that "today's date must fall between January 1 and December 31" is true. How does that help me figure out what today's date actually is? The temptation that Aristotle wants to avoid is always putting the mean in the exact middle between the two extremes. In the same way that we do not want to conclude that the date is always July 1, because that's the middle between January 1 and December 31, we also do not want to conclude that courage lies exactly in the middle between cowardice and rashness. But where does it lie? Aristotle notes that, in most cases, the mean doesn't lie in the exact middle; it lies closer to one of the extremes. Let's think about courage again. Does courage look more like rashness or like cowardice? Or we could put the question this way: Would you rather be known as cowardly or rash? I think most people would rather be thought of as rash, and indeed, most acts of courage look a lot more like rashness than they do cowardice. So, in the case of fear, the mean lies closer to deficiency than excess (EN II.6, 1105a–1106b35; EN II.9, 1109a1–20). Our picture now looks like this:

Cowardice   Courage   Rashness

The issue is even more complicated than this, though. Even if courage is generally closer to rashness, surely it will not be in the exact same spot every time. Take basketball, for example. In order to make a basket, I will have to vary my shot a great deal. A three-pointer requires more effort than a lay-up. There is no one size fits all answer here. I hit the mark when I exert myself to the right degree, at the right time, at the right place. Even courage will move closer or farther from rashness, depending on the situation. Habits are not reflexes or instincts. They are complex and supple. Good basketball players are always modulating their habits to play well, to hit the mark. In the same way, courageous people are attuned to their situation so that they can exert themselves to the right degree (EN II.9, 1109a25–30).

The mean is relative to us

Aristotle also recognizes that people are different and that these differences will lead to differences in means. What might be a praiseworthy action for me on the basketball court would be laughable coming from LeBron James. What a soldier might consider courageous on the battlefield would be rash for me. This is not to say, however, that all actions are virtuous. Just because people are different does not mean that anything goes. Our differences mean that the standard is determined by who we are, but we can still fall short of that standard. Developing bad habits is always an option, and the only defense against bad habits is good habits. If our habits are bad, then the actions that follow from them will be blameworthy, no matter who we are. If our habits are good, then the actions that follow from them will be praiseworthy. When we are acting on our good habits we flourish (EN II.8, 1108b).

It may seem as if Aristotle comes very close here to affirming ethical relativism, the idea that each person has a unique ethics. The corollary that is usually added to this is that no one can make judgments about another person's ethics. Neither ethical relativism nor its corollary is true for Aristotle. Ethical relativism is false for two reasons. First, while there may be subtle variations at the margins about particular virtuous acts, it is never the case that virtue can be found in excess or deficiency. Courage is always behaving rationally with regard to one's fear. Reason may dictate an increased or decreased response to fear, depending on the situation, but the result would never be that it would be reasonable to be rash or cowardly in any situation. Second, for Aristotle, this limited flexibility with regard to moral virtue follows from the nature of ethics itself. All areas of inquiry have a level of precision that is appropriate to them. Mathematics requires a high degree of precision. History, simply because of the nature of its object, cannot be as precise. To treat history with the same precision as mathematics would lead to a certainty unwarranted by historical research. By the same token, it does not follow from this difference in precision that we can say whatever we want about historical events and be right. Ethics admits of less precision than other areas of inquiry. It is more like history than mathematics, and doing it right requires recognizing this (EN I.3, 1094b20–5).

If ethical relativism is false, then its corollary is obviously false. But let's take a moment to see where exactly the problem lies. For Aristotle, the reason ethical judgments are possible, the reason we can rightly praise or blame people for their actions, is reason itself. If I see a plant with dry, yellowing leaves, I immediately infer that it is not flourishing. Furthermore, its lack of flourishing must be related to its form or shape. It is not flourishing because it is not growing or taking in nutrients well. I do not say, "This plant really is flourishing. It's just that this plant's flourishing doesn't involve growing and taking in nutrients." Plant flourishing is not relative, though differences in the way this flourishing is expressed among plants do exist, and I can rightly judge that this is the case. In the same way, I can clearly see when a person is not flourishing. Furthermore, for Aristotle, this failure to flourish must arise from an inability to use reason to properly control the actions and emotions. I can make this judgment as surely as I can make the judgment that a jump shot that misses its mark is a bad shot. The issue is not whether I can understand why a person missed the shot, bad pass, good defense, etc. The issue is whether I would imitate that action, make it a habit. Reason makes this judgment.

Intellectual virtues are *not* acquired by habit

Unlike the moral virtues, which are habits to control the actions and emotions of our animal souls, the intellectual virtues are acquired through learning. Again, if we take mathematics as our example, this becomes clear. I can imitate a mathematics professor very precisely. I can draw numbers, variables, exponents, and formulas exactly as she does. I might even be praised for my excellent penmanship, but unless what I am writing down is actually explained, I will never learn how to do mathematics. Aristotle recognizes that there is a whole set of actions that are not amenable to habituation. Aristotle also recognizes that these actions are related to thinking. He concludes from this that there are virtues related to thinking that are different in kind from the moral virtues. He calls these other virtues "intellectual virtues" (EN II.1, 1103a15–17).

Another important way that intellectual virtues differ from moral virtues is their number. Since moral virtues are the excellences of actions and emotions, the number of moral virtues is practically unlimited. For (almost) any action or emotion you can think of, there is a right way to do it that lies somewhere between excess and deficiency. Since intellectual virtues concern thinking, it might seem as if there should be even more of them than the moral virtues. My actions and emotions are restricted in ways that my thoughts are not. While Aristotle recognizes this, at the same time, he thinks that there are five basic ways to think excellently. These five basic ways of thinking excellently are the intellectual virtues:

1. Art
2. Practical wisdom
3. Intelligence
4. Scientific knowledge
5. Theoretical wisdom. (EN VI.3, 1139b12–16)

Intellectual virtues are ways of telling the truth

Since the moral virtues are concerned with the right amount of effort, it is easy to see why that would be found somewhere on a continuum between too much and too little. Thinking does not work quite that way, though. While we might talk about thinking being hard or easy, its virtue does not lie here. Its virtue lies in getting at the truth. If I am working on a mathematical problem, no one cares how hard I worked. I can even imagine working hard being a sign of deficiency. What matters, what is praiseworthy or blameworthy, is whether I got the answer right. Did I tell the truth about the problem? I only think excellently when I am getting at the truth of things. For Aristotle, truth does not come in degrees. It is binary. A thought is either true or false, and there is no in between (EN VI.3, 1139b12–16).

Even if we agree with Aristotle that truth does not come in degrees, does it not follow that there is only one truth? Why does Aristotle think there are five ways of telling the truth? To begin answering this question let's think about the kinds of things that we can think about. Aristotle thinks we can group all the possible objects of thought, or ideas, into two basic groups: things that *can* be otherwise and things that *cannot* be otherwise. This may seem like a strange way to group things, but maybe a few examples will help. We are obviously familiar with things that can be otherwise. There are multiple ways for me to drive to work in the morning. The best way to get to work will depend on a whole host of other factors. Whichever way I do go, though, I could have always taken a different route. The sentence that I am typing right now could be written with different words in a different order and still convey the same meaning. That sentence could have been otherwise than it is. All of the things we can think about that could be other than they are, we call "contingent" (EN VI.1, 1139a5–10).

What about things that cannot be otherwise? We might be hard pressed initially to come up with anything in this category. What is there that could not be otherwise? What about triangles? Could it be otherwise that the interior angles of a triangle add up to 180 degrees? Is that not an unchanging truth about the nature of triangles that cannot be otherwise? What about the Pythagorean theorem? Is it always the case that $a^2 + b^2 = c^2$? While we do not encounter these objects that cannot be otherwise as physical objects, it turns out that there are quite a few really important things that cannot be otherwise. We call these objects "necessary" (EN VI.1, 1139a5–10).

Of the five intellectual virtues, two tell the truth about objects that can be otherwise – art and practical wisdom; two tell the truth about objects that cannot be otherwise – scientific knowledge and theoretical wisdom; and one – intelligence – has a role to play with regard to both kinds of objects (EN VI.1, 1139a6–10). We can map out the relations this way:

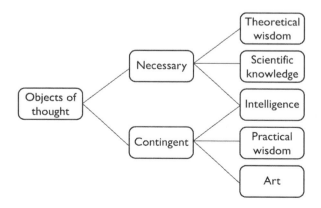

For Aristotle, "art" is a much broader category than it is for us. It includes anything crafted by human hands from digging ditches to a sculpture of Athena. Art is telling the truth about things made. There is a right way and a wrong way to build a chair, for example. "Right way," however, does not mean singular. The right way to build a chair is to build a chair appropriate to the situation. This is where "thinking about things that can be otherwise" is really important (EN VI.4, 1140a1–24).

Practical wisdom is deliberating well about what to do. It means doing the right thing for the right reason. Not only does practical wisdom require that we take note of all the immediate circumstances, but it also requires that we consider whether or not a given action is in keeping with our overall flourishing. This kind of deliberation is a process of reasoning that Aristotle calls a "practical syllogism" (EN VI.5, 1140a24–1140b5): that is, a valid argument for the best action to take in any given situation. Let's take a look at the kind of thing that Aristotle has in mind:

Health is good (i.e., conducive to flourishing).
Eating dark, leafy greens is healthy.
Here are some dark, leafy greens.
Eat them!

Practical wisdom does two things here. First, it provides the premises about the goodness of health and the fact that dark, leafy greens are healthy. The second thing practical wisdom does, is that it draws the inference that it would be best to eat the dark, leafy greens. Most of the time this kind of deliberation happens so quickly that we barely notice. It comes to the fore, though, when we face big, life-altering decisions, such as choosing a college or a major. For Aristotle, we cannot flourish unless we do this kind of deliberation well (EN VI.7, 1141b15–21).

Notice in the above example, though, that practical wisdom does not provide all the premises for deliberation. Identifying the actual presence of dark, leafy greens is the task of intelligence. Intelligence "grasps particulars" so that practical wisdom can draw an inference about the best course of action. Telling the truth about what to do requires more than platitudes about health. It requires something, a particular, that can be acted on. The role of intelligence with regard to things that can be otherwise is to provide particulars (this, here, now) that are necessary for practical wisdom to complete its deliberations (EN VI.7, 1141b15).

Intelligence does something similar with regard to objects of thought that cannot be otherwise. Here it grasps first or fundamental principles, principles that cannot be deduced but must simply be known. An example of a principle in this category is the principle of non-contradiction, which states that A ≠ non-A. Something cannot be both itself and its opposite at the same time. If I hold the position that fire both burns and does not burn, or that water is both wet and not wet, I become incapable of telling the truth about anything, since everything is both itself and not itself. Furthermore, it is very difficult to convince me otherwise, since any arguments would already presuppose the principle of non-contradiction. This principle is something I either see or do not. Aristotle calls this way of telling the truth "intelligence" (EN VI.6, 1141a7).

Given the fundamental principles grasped by intelligence, theoretical wisdom draws inferences from these principles to produce new conclusions about things that cannot be otherwise. Thus, theoretical wisdom deliberates in a way that is analogous to practical wisdom, but the object of deliberation differs. Scientific knowledge takes the principles of intelligence and the deliberations of theoretical wisdom and organizes them systematically. Thus, scientific wisdom is telling the truth about the way that knowledge of necessary things is organized. Scientific wisdom takes, for example, the truths gleaned about space from intelligence and theoretical wisdom, and organizes them into geometry (EN VI.7, 1141a15–21).

We might quibble with the way Aristotle divides things up here, but let's not lose sight of his fundamental task. Flourishing is acting in accord with reason, and we can reason in some very distinct ways. In order to discover what flourishing is, we first have to understand these distinct ways of reasoning. For Aristotle, there are five distinct ways of reasoning. They are distinguished by their object and their task. Flourishing means performing these tasks well.

Pleasure and the highest happiness

While most people would agree with Aristotle that pleasure is not the most important thing in life, the question of pleasure's relation to human flourishing remains open until the end of the *Nicomachean Ethics*. Here Aristotle argues (not surprisingly) that pleasure is neither wholly good nor wholly bad. More importantly, though, he argues that pleasure is not good in itself but is only good insofar as it accompanies good action. If I take pleasure in a bad act – say, stealing, then the pleasure that accompanies that act is also bad. If I take pleasure in being courageous, then that pleasure is good. Aristotle even goes so far as to say that those who do not take pleasure in virtuous acts do not really possess the virtue (EN I.8, 1099a17). No one who is forced to act virtuously, or begrudgingly acts virtuously, is really flourishing. Ultimately, Aristotle's position on pleasure is that flourishing is pleasurable, but that no one flourishes for the sake of pleasure. Thus, flourishing and pleasure are distinct, and flourishing is the highest good (EN X.5, 1175b24–30).

In the remainder of the book Aristotle wonders if there are different kinds of flourishing, and whether these can be ranked. Given Aristotle's mania for categorizing, it is not surprising that he thinks there are different kinds of flourishing. The flourishing associated with acting according to the moral virtues differs from the flourishing associated with acting according to the intellectual virtues. Even within the intellectual virtues, the flourishing associated with telling the truth about things that cannot change differs from the flourishing associated with telling the truth about things that can change. Can these differences be ranked, though? Is one kind of flourishing superior to another? Aristotle says, "Yes" (EN X.7, 1177a12–17).

The reason that Aristotle thinks that some kinds of flourishing are superior to others is rooted in his conception of soul as the form of a living thing. The flourishing associated with the intellectual virtues is superior to the flourishing associated with the moral virtues precisely because the locus of the intellectual virtues in human reason is superior to the locus of the moral virtues in the animal soul. It is extraordinarily important to note that Aristotle does not think the moral virtues are bad. No, they remain essential to a life well lived. But, if we are asking what kind of actions better exemplify human flourishing, Aristotle's response is those actions in accord with the intellectual virtues (EN X.7, 1177a18–35).

Aristotle applies the same kind of reasoning to the differences in flourishing within the intellectual virtues. Which is superior, though, the theoretical intellectual virtues or the practical intellectual virtues? The practical intellectual virtues (art, practical wisdom, intelligence) may seem like the obvious choice. Knowing what to do and how to make things seems way more important than the esoteric knowledge of unchanging things. Aristotle argues, though, that it is precisely the difference in object (changing versus unchanging) that makes the flourishing associated with the theoretical intellectual virtues (theoretical wisdom, scientific knowledge, intelligence) superior. Deciding which major to declare may seem of all-consuming importance, but does it really compare to the unchanging majesty of the Pythagorean theorem? Not for Aristotle. The eternal, necessary objects contemplated by the theoretical intellect are superior to the contingent, fleeting objects pursued by the practical intellect. In fact, Aristotle says that in pursuing the theoretical intellectual virtues, or "contemplation," we come as close as possible to transcending our humanity and becoming godlike. Flourishing like the gods is superior to any other kind of flourishing (EN X.7, 1177b26–1178a3).

Aristotle recognizes that few will reach this pinnacle, but that it is still worth pursuing as the very best of which we are capable. Even if we do not reach these heights, though, a life of flourishing is still available to us. All that it requires is acting according to the best part of who we are. In the case of our actions and emotions, this means using reason to develop good habits. In the case of our intellect, this means telling the truth about the different objects of thought. Acting excellently in every facet of life is the key to flourishing, the key to happiness, the key to a life well lived.

Summary

Happiness is an activity of the soul in accordance with virtue. Moral virtues are acquired by habit. Intellectual virtues are telling the truth. The highest happiness is found in contemplation, the exercise of the theoretical intellectual virtues.

Questions

1. Do you think the best kind of life is the contemplation of/ telling the truth about what does not change?
2. How important are habits in education/character formation?
3. What did Aristotle get right and wrong about a life well lived?

3

Spinoza: The Universe and Power
(*Ethics*, Parts 1, 2, and 3)

Key terms

Substance – That which everything is a part of. The whole. The universe. God.

Mode – The parts of the whole. Humans are all modes.

Affect – Any interaction of modes.

Emotion – Affects that most concern human behavior. Love, hate, etc.

Power – Ability or capacity.

Despite the fact that Aristotle writes in Ancient Greece while Spinoza writes at the dawn of the modern era in seventeenth-century Holland, both are trying to answer the same question, How should we live? They even agree that a life well lived is a life lived according to reason. They will disagree profoundly, however, about the meaning of "according to reason" and, consequently, the nature of a life well lived. While Aristotle confirms many of our intuitions about excellent thought and action, Spinoza will challenge many of our most basic assumptions about human nature and the world we live in. As always, our task is not simply to agree or disagree with Spinoza, but to figure out where we stand and why. It is only by testing our mettle against other thinkers that we can hone our own philosophy.

The idiot in the SUV

Let's begin our discussion of Spinoza with a brief story. I do not like SUVs. I think there are very few circumstances in which one actually needs an SUV. SUVs are not appropriate for driving in a city, and yet I seem beset on all sides by SUVs. While getting cut off by any car makes me angry, you can imagine how angry I would become if an SUV cut me off. I would fume and curse and spin the most delicious revenge fantasies in my head. Let's suppose that while I am placating myself with this imaginary revenge and staring daggers into the SUV, I watch it turn into a hospital parking lot. Once in the parking lot, the driver jumps out and runs to the passenger door. He opens the door and helps out a very pregnant woman. A nurse runs out with a wheelchair, and they all rush into the hospital. What happens to my anger at this point? Is it still possible to be angry now that I see why I was cut off? I may feel other emotions at this point, maybe guilt and shame, but anger does not really seem like an option any more. Why? Is the disappearance of my anger not correlated exactly with the increase in my understanding? The second I realize, "Oh, that's why he cut me off," is the second I am no longer angry. For Spinoza, this "understanding why" is the key to a life well lived.

God, the universe, and causality

So many questions arise at this point. What does Spinoza mean by "understanding"? How does it compare to the intellectual virtues in Aristotle? What about the moral virtues? What about habit? What about pleasure? In order to answer these questions and better understand Spinoza in his own right, let's take a look at his metaphysics. We will see that Spinoza's ethics follow from his metaphysics, precisely as Aristotle's did. We will also see that insofar as Spinoza's metaphysics differ from Aristotle, his ethics differ, too.

The key to Spinoza's metaphysics is his view of the universe. He thinks the universe is a single, interconnected whole. Nothing lies outside of the universe, and the reason for anything being the way it is in the universe is its connection to other parts of the universe. The reason there are mountains outside my window is plate tectonics. The reason that I have a window facing the mountains is the result of an architect's decision over a century ago, and the fact that this is the office that was available when I arrived here. Spinoza has many names for this interconnected whole. Sometimes he calls it "nature." Sometimes he calls it "substance." Sometimes, much to the chagrin of some of his early readers, he calls it "God." Claiming that the universe and God are the same thing is called "pantheism." This distinguishes Spinoza's view that God *is* everything from the more traditional idea that God is *in* everything. God being in everything is compatible with Christianity, but pantheism is not, and it was really frowned upon in Spinoza's day. By "frowned upon," I mean it is the kind of thing that could get you burned at the stake, even in seventeenth-century Europe. For the sake of clarity, we will stick to "universe" as much as possible, and feel free whenever you see the word "God" in the *Ethics* to replace it with "universe." This will prevent you from bringing too many preconceived ideas to Spinoza's text (E1P11 and P14).[1]

If the universe is a single, interconnected whole, how do we talk about the parts of that whole? The word that Spinoza uses to talk about the parts of the whole is "mode." Everything is a "mode" or "modification" of the whole. That is, Spinoza's whole is constantly changing as its interconnected parts interact with one another. For Spinoza, these modes interact according to the law of cause and effect. There are no causes without effects, and no effects without causes. It is hard to find anything to disagree with at this point, but we need to dig a littler further into this notion of cause and effect. What exactly is the nature of the relation between cause and effect? There are two possible answers here – and these should be familiar from our discussion of Aristotle: necessary and contingent. Either effects follow their

---

[1] Like Aristotle, Spinoza also has a standard reference system for citations, regardless of the edition. In this case, the "E" indicates the *Ethics*. The number immediately following "E" indicates which of the five parts of the *Ethics* the citation is referring to. So, "E1" means "*Ethics*, Part One." Spinoza's work is further divided into definitions, axioms, and propositions. Here, the citation "E1P11 and P14" means that the information in the preceding paragraph can be found in *Ethics*, Part One, Propositions 11 and 14. The propositions are also further divided into proofs and scholia, which comment on the proposition. Thus, in the citation "E1P11Proof" refers to *Ethics*, Part One, Proposition 11, Proof, and "E1P11S" refers to the scholium of the same proposition. All of the quotations in the chapters on Spinoza refer to Spinoza, *The Essential Spinoza: Ethics and Related Writings*, trans. Samuel Shirley (Indianapolis: Hackett, 2006).

causes *necessarily* and thus *cannot* be otherwise, or effects follow their
causes contingently and *can* be otherwise (E1Def5).

In order to think through these possibilities, let's take a simple
example: I drop a pen on the floor. The pen bounces and lands a
few feet away from me perpendicular to the way I am facing. Given
the cause (my dropping the pen), is the effect (where the pen lands)
necessary or contingent? The immediate and tempting answer is that
where the pen lands is contingent. In fact, it is easy to demonstrate.
I can drop the pen a hundred times and it would not end up in the
same spot. Surely this demonstrates that effects follow their causes
contingently. But does it really? I can see very clearly that the effects
are different, but why exactly are they different? Have I taken care
to ensure that the causes are exactly the same? Remember the issue
is not whether similar causes (dropping the pen) will produce identical effects (pen landing in the exactly the same place), but whether
the exact cause (dropping the same pen, from the same height, in
the same place, under identical conditions) will produce the same
effect. So, which is the better conclusion here: that effects follow
their causes contingently, or that slight variations in causes produce
slightly different effects? Would science even be possible on the first
conclusion? Could a scientist say, "I ran this experiment twice, and
it gave me two different results. That's what I expected since effects
follow their causes contingently." Or would we expect a scientist to
say, "I ran this experiment twice and got two different results. There
must be a problem with the way I set up the experiment, because
I expect the exact same causes to produce the exact same results
every time." Claims like this indicate that the relation between cause
and effect is necessary. The appearance of contingency is, in fact,
slightly different causes producing slightly different effects. The pen
lands three inches to the left because I held the pen slightly differently. For Spinoza, the connections among all the modes of the universe are necessary connections (E1P28).

Free will

Everything in the universe is connected. The nature of that connection is necessary; things could not have been otherwise than they are.
This is all well and good for things. We can see that science crucially

depends on this assumption to carry out its experiments, but what about people? Is Spinoza claiming that human action is also governed by the law of necessary cause and effect? Yes, this is exactly what Spinoza is claiming. This is the first place that Spinoza is really going to challenge our intuitions about human nature. Free will is an illusion for Spinoza (E3P2S). Furthermore, belief in free will lies at the root of many of our problems. It is one of the main reasons we fail to flourish. Spinoza's reasoning here is straightforward:

> Every effect in the universe follows its cause with necessity.
> Humans are part of the universe.
> Human actions are also part of the necessary chain of cause and effect.

The implications of Spinoza's position are radical. Everything we have ever done, from choosing a college to the shirt we put on this morning, was necessary. It could not have been otherwise. While human action is obviously more complex, the mechanics are identical to dropping the pen. The reason why the pen lands in one place and not another depends on the pen and how I drop it. Any change in those conditions will have a different result. In the same way, choosing a college or putting on a shirt are the necessary effects of a chain of causes. I chose this shirt *because* I like the way it looks. I chose this college *because* it gave me the best financial aid package. For Spinoza, the fact that we can see multiple options in our future and remember those options after we have chosen creates the illusion that we could have chosen otherwise. But we could no more have chosen otherwise than the pen, given its initial starting conditions, could have landed elsewhere (E3P2S).

For Spinoza, claiming that necessary causality works for everything in the universe but humans either misunderstands causality or it misunderstands the universe. A cause that does not determine its effect is not a cause. It may be the case, for example, that I do not fully understand why I chose the shirt that I did this morning. The cause may be complex, combining many motivations – what is clean, what is comfortable, what matches other things I am wearing, when I wore it last, etc. There are surely others that I am only dimly aware of, or perhaps not even aware of at all. Spinoza wants to caution us that, just because we have incomplete information about a cause, it does not follow from this that an additional power (a free will, for example) intervenes to fill in the gap. A poorly understood or unknown cause is still a cause. We do not get to fill in the gap in our knowledge with some secret entity (E3P2S).

Exempting humans from necessary causality misunderstands the universe, because it supposes that some force or power lies outside the universe in order to be exempt from the laws of the universe. As we have seen, for Spinoza, the "universe" is simply the name for all that is. By definition, nothing can lie outside the universe. If we posit some kind of limit for the universe and then posit something beyond that limit, in effect all we have done is expanded the limits of the universe. The real problem of positing something outside the limits of the universe is ultimately a problem of interaction. How can something outside the universe have an effect on something inside the universe? Specifically, what would be the mechanism for this interaction? It looks like this extra-universal power would need to commandeer the power of the universe (i.e., causality), in which case the extra-universal power becomes part of the universe and works according to necessary causality. Or the extra-universal power would remain pristinely separate and thus unable to interact with anything in the universe. Either way, it seems that there is no room for anything like free will to give us absolute power over our choices (E1P26).

Ethics without free will

Not only does Spinoza thumb his nose at one of our most cherished notions, free will, but also it leaves him with a really difficult problem to solve. Without free will, there is no responsibility. How is ethics possible without responsibility? As we saw, Aristotle was supremely concerned with notions of praiseworthiness and blameworthiness. These assume that we are, in fact, responsible for our actions. On Spinoza's view, responsibility evaporates. We cannot be responsible for our actions, because we could not have acted in any other way. Whatever shape Spinoza's ethics finally takes, it must be an ethics that does not depend on a notion of responsibility and free will.

Wait! What about criminals? Is Spinoza saying that we should open all the jails because people are not responsible for the crimes for which they have been convicted? There are two claims here, a claim about responsibility and a claim about what should be done to those who damage society. Spinoza is saying that people are not responsible for anything, even crimes. We must be clear, though, that, by "responsible," Spinoza means "could have acted otherwise." Does it follow from this, though, that we should let such people run free and continue to do whatever they wish? Does the fact that someone commits a crime mean that we must continue letting that person commit crimes? Absolutely not. If people are acting in a way that is damaging to society, this seems like a sufficient reason to stop them and, as far as possible, prevent them from committing future acts that are damaging to society. Responsibility is irrelevant here. We simply need to identify harm and seek to prevent it (E4P18S).

Identifying harm and seeking to prevent it is at the heart of Spinoza's ethics. Such an ethics does not require free will or responsibility. It only requires understanding. For Spinoza, to the degree that I understand the universe, the things in the universe, and myself, I will live well. To suppose that I have free will is to misunderstand myself, and thus misunderstand what I am capable of. If we return to the story above about the idiot in the SUV, we can see this very clearly. When the SUV first cuts me off, why am I mad? The tempting answer is that I am mad because I was cut off. A little reflection, though, shows that this really is not the case. I am mad because I assume that I did not have to be cut off. My assumption is that the driver has free will and therefore could have acted otherwise. Since he could have acted otherwise but did not, he is responsible and blameworthy for his actions. In a scenario where someone wrongs me and I impute free will to that person, I am bound to become angry precisely because I believe that person could have acted otherwise. When I see the reason why I was cut off, when I see that the driver could not have acted otherwise, my anger disappears. What about my guilt and shame over my anger? Are these not simply the result of imputing free will to myself? I feel bad about being angry, as if I could have acted otherwise. For Spinoza, I cannot live well unless I see things clearly. Free will is an illusion that obscures this kind of clarity (E45P50S).

The emotions

While Aristotle and Spinoza both think that controlling the emotions is necessary for human flourishing, they understand the emotions and the nature of their control differently. As we saw, for Aristotle, emotions are located in our animal soul and controlled through the acquisition of good habits. While Spinoza does not deny the importance of good habits in living well, his view of human nature is so different that good habits are no longer the main focus. For Spinoza, everything follows from his view of the universe as all the necessary interconnections among the parts or modes of the universe. Part Three of Spinoza's *Ethics* is a taxonomy of possible connections.

Let's take a little time to think about what this might mean. I am constantly interacting with the world in ways that are both conscious and unconscious. Right now I am typing on a keyboard. I am simultaneously affecting the keyboard, while being affected by the keyboard. At the same time, I am reading what I am writing. Sometimes it seems as if my fingers are moving to correct errors before I even realize that I have made an error. The light shining in my window is creating a slight glare on my glasses, but for the most part I ignore it. While I am not really conscious of it, my body is metabolizing my breakfast to turn it into sugars for energy and nutrients to maintain proper cellular functioning. I could, no doubt, fill this entire book simply cataloging the myriad ways that I am affecting the world and being affected by it.

Spinoza recognizes this vast complexity and wonders if there is any way that some order can be imposed on it. He argues that, despite the immense array of possible interconnections, they can all be boiled down to three basic ways of interacting with the world: pleasure, pain, and striving. In order to understand why Spinoza is able to reduce all of our interactions to three basic ones, we need to think in terms of power. "Power," for Spinoza, simply means "ability" or "capacity." The basic insight here is that some of the ways that we interact with the world increase our power, and some of the ways that we interact with the world decrease our power. Understanding the difference is the key to living well for Spinoza (E3Def3).

In order to illustrate the way in which interactions affect my capacities, let's look at a few examples. Suppose that I fell asleep with my neck at a strange angle. Here I have an interaction between my head and the pillow. When I awake the next morning I have a crick in my neck and a splitting headache. How do I function for the rest of the day? To be honest, I am a little surly. I am averse to noise and bright lights, and I have a difficult time getting work done, because the headache prevents me from concentrating. I also find that I am holding my head at an odd angle to try to alleviate some of the pressure on my neck and head. I find it painful to look both ways when I cross the street. Has the interaction with my pillow increased or decreased my power? Am I more or less capable than I was the day before, when I had a good night's sleep? It seems obvious to me, as I stumble around in a fog with shooting pains every time I turn my head, that my power has decreased. Because my power has decreased, Spinoza would say that the emotions arising from this head–pillow interaction are rooted in the basic emotion of pain. My surliness, my foggy-headedness, my sensitivity to light and sound, all of these are indications that my ability to interact with the world is diminished (E3P13S).

What is my response? I can imagine lots of things happening here. I could wallow in self-pity and go back to bed with a cold compress over my eyes. I could take an aspirin. Maybe I could have an extra cup of tea in the morning in an attempt to ward off some of the fogginess. That is, I can give in to my diminished power or I can seek to overcome it as much as possible. To the degree that I give in to my diminished power, I am not living well. To the degree that I seek to restore and increase my power, I am living well. Maybe you are thinking, "Hey, wait a minute. Did Spinoza just secretly sneak free will in the back door here?" It might be tempting to think that, but no. He is not saying that you *should* choose to increase your power, and if you fail to, then you are blameworthy, because you could have chosen otherwise. Rather, Spinoza is saying that *if* you pursue an increase in your power, then you will live well. Spinoza is simply describing the nature of things. Those who increase their power live well. Those who do not, do not. The "if" here, like any other effect in Spinoza's universe, is utterly dependent on prior causes.

It is pretty easy to see how pain decreases our power. In the same way, it is also easy to see how pleasure increases our power. If I sleep well the night after the headache, I have a much, much better day. What about the third type of interaction, striving? Spinoza says that striving is the essence of all things. It is the tendency of all things to preserve themselves. That is, some of the interactions that we engage in enable us to stay alive. Some of these interactions are basic, such as air, food, water, and shelter. If we cannot combine with these, we perish pretty quickly. The fact is, though, that nobody eats "food." We only eat particular kinds of food. Thus, understanding is required to combine with those foods that best preserve our nature. Even here, there will be important differences. Peanut butter might be a life-saving protein in some instances, but it is deadly to someone with a severe peanut allergy. If I wish to flourish, I must understand the difference between those things that preserve my nature and those things that decompose my nature (E3P6).

Return of the idiot in the SUV

Using what we know about Spinoza, let's return to the example of being cut off by the SUV. What happens to my power if I'm cut off while driving? Surely, this is a decrease. I have to swerve or stop abruptly to avoid being hit. I can no longer drive as I was driving before. My capacities are limited. More importantly, though, what happens to me? I become angry. Anger is an interesting emotion for Spinoza. It is the desire to destroy an object of hatred. I hate whatever causes me pain, whatever decreases my power. In an effort to regain my power, I become angry. For the most part, the desire to destroy an object of hatred is impotent, which is why I indulge in fantasies of revenge. Sometimes, though, we actually do destroy objects of hatred. Have you ever felt a mosquito bite you, only to discover it still sucking blood from your leg? Do you smash it in a bloody mess on your leg? That's hatred leading to an anger that destroys the object of its hatred. In the case of the SUV, though, my anger destroys only an imaginary object, not the real thing (E3P39).

Why are hatred and anger a decrease in my power, though? There is no question that both are emotions arising out of pain, but why do they block flourishing? When I am angry, my whole world revolves around the object of my hatred. All my thoughts are consumed by my anger and directed toward the object causing me pain. For the most part, I am wondering why this is happening to me and imagining the hated object acting differently. While all of this is happening, I am manifestly not concerned with my own preservation. In fact, either through distraction or rashness, I might put myself in serious danger. While staring daggers at the SUV I might run into the back of another car. In my anger I might start an altercation with the SUV driver. The fact of the matter is that nursing my grudge leads me away from flourishing rather than toward it (E3P55).

Once I see the SUV turn into the hospital, I might run through emotions such as guilt and shame (E3Def. of Emotions31). Both of these emotions arise out of pain and are connected to imagining that things could have been otherwise. This kind of thinking, however, is detrimental to understanding and, as a result, prevents flourishing. When I finally do drive away, understanding why I was cut off in the first place, my anger dissipates. To the degree that it dissipates, my thoughts and actions become my own again. I am no longer distracted or tempted to rash actions. My path toward preservation and flourishing is no longer blocked. At this point, to the degree that I understand, I am striving.

The development of Spinoza's philosophy corresponds with the rise of what we would recognize as modern science. His great task is to articulate an ethics in keeping with the strictures of an interconnected world and the iron necessity of cause and effect. Such an ethics can no longer depend on human uniqueness grounded in free will. Without these traditional constraints on ethics, Spinoza centers his theory on the emotions as ways in which we affect and are affected by our environment. The key to flourishing or striving is to understand the ways in which we can be affected and as much as possible combine with things that increase our power rather than decrease it. In the next chapter, we will turn to the hindrances to increasing our power and the understanding required to increase our power.

Summary

The universe is an interconnected system governed by necessary causality. Humans are part of this system and thus have no free will. They do, however, have the ability to understand the universe. Freedom lies in the understanding.

Questions
1. Both Spinoza and Aristotle agree that reason is the key to living well. Do you agree?
2. Given advances in science, does it make sense to talk about "free will"?
3. How is ethics possible without free will?

4

Spinoza: Emotions and Freedom
(*Ethics*, Parts 4 and 5)

Key terms

Freedom – Understanding oneself, things, and the universe.
Bondage – Being determined by causes opposed to one's nature.
Virtue – Power.
Reason – Seeing the necessary interconnection of things.
Intuition – Understanding that whatever is the case could not have been otherwise.

Why do good people do bad things? Why do we see the better path but follow the worse? These are questions that any philosophy needs to answer. Plato thought that the answer to these questions was ignorance. He thought that anyone who truly understood the good would always seek it. Or, to put it another way, no one knowingly does evil. This idea does not quite square with our own experience, though. It seems as if we often knowingly do things that are damaging to us or those around us. Take a simple example such as dessert. Most of the time we know that we would be better off without dessert, but we eat it anyway in full knowledge of its detrimental effects. Here, it looks as if the problem is not ignorance. Aristotle tries to solve this problem in a slightly different way. As we saw, knowledge is really important for Aristotle, but he also recognizes that knowledge may not be enough. Sometimes it is our will that may fall short. We may fully understand that eating dessert right now is a bad move but have an insufficiently strong will to control ourselves.

Spinoza also takes on these questions explicitly in his *Ethics*, but answers them differently from both Plato and Aristotle. In distinction from Plato, he clearly thinks that one can see the better path but not seek it. In distinction from Aristotle, Spinoza does not think that the reason one might fail to follow the better path arises from weakness of the will. As we have already seen, the will is not free for Spinoza; it is always necessarily determined by prior causes. In this necessary determination lies Spinoza's answer to the question of good people doing bad things. We do bad things, regardless of our knowledge, when our past causes necessarily lead to that effect. Spinoza calls this seeing the better path but following the worse "bondage."

Bondage

For Spinoza, we are in bondage anytime our past causes determine us in a way that is detrimental to our striving. There is no praise or blame here. Spinoza is simply describing human behavior. People often act in ways that are damaging to themselves. Why? Furthermore, people often act in ways that are damaging to themselves, knowing full well that they are acting this way. Here Spinoza is pointing to all of those times that we feel like a helpless observer to our own actions. "I know this is wrong. I don't want to do this, but here I am doing it anyway." While I am fuming about the driver in the SUV who cut me off, I may have a brief moment of clarity in which I question the helpfulness of the revenge fantasy to which I keep adding more and more detail. The moment of clarity quickly fades, though, as my emotions overwhelm my reason. Bondage is losing control of myself and failing to act in my own best interest (E4Preface).

We can illustrate this possibility in numerous ways. Where I teach, it is a tradition for students to take each other out drinking on their twenty-first birthday. From what I have heard, this rarely has salutary effects. The student celebrating her birthday is put in a situation where she is pressured to drink a great deal of alcohol quickly. Two things happen. First, even if she might think better of drinking so much on a different occasion, her friends will say, "C'mon! It's your birthday." Second, the more she drinks, the more her capacity for clear thinking diminishes. The result of these intertwining causes is that, even if on another occasion she might have refused the fifth Jägerbomb, in this situation her causes determined her to drink it (E4P3).

Or suppose that I arrive at college and for the first few weeks I get along famously with my roommate. In the fourth week, though, he starts dating someone. The change in his personality is almost immediate. He is completely obsessed with his new significant other. He spends all of his time texting and snapchatting with her. He stops doing his homework, and he stops hanging out with his original group of friends. He becomes surly and distant. He begins dressing differently and talking differently. In short, he has become a different person. He is certainly not the same roommate I had when we moved in together. What accounts for the change in my roommate? He is connecting with the world differently. He is engaging in new combinations. These new combinations are creating new causes, which are leading to new effects. Spinoza's only question is Are these new combinations increasing or decreasing his power? If they are decreasing his power, it is bondage (E4P5).

Escape

Given Spinoza's view of the universe, are we not simply doomed? If what happens could not have happened in any other way, why try? No matter what we do, it will always be the necessary result of past causes. How can Spinoza pretend to have anything like an ethics without something like free will to intervene? Will we not always be in bondage with no possibility of escape? There is no question that Spinoza has a lot to answer for here, but let's think through what he is saying. He is absolutely committed to the proposition that effects follow their causes with necessity. He is committed to this, even for really complex causes like human behavior. Thus, there is no free will. The really important question that Spinoza needs to answer is, Is change possible without free will? That is, is it possible to escape bondage, or are we doomed to repeat the same mistakes over and over again (E4P20)?

On one level, the question is really easy to answer. We can simply look at experience. Do we repeat the same mistakes over and over again? Usually not. We have lots of sayings that indicate our ability to change our behavior based on past mistakes, such as "Once bitten, twice shy" and "Fool me once. Shame on you. Fool me twice. Shame on me." There is clearly an expectation that we can and should learn from our mistakes. We do not always learn, but it looks as if learning is possible.

On another level, the question becomes more difficult. Even if Spinoza grants that learning from our mistakes is possible, how is it possible? Here is where, Spinoza would say, an intractable belief in free will gets in the way. Suppose the student who goes drinking on her twenty-first birthday wakes up the next morning with an apocalyptic hangover. She resolves from that point forward that three Jägerbombs is her absolute limit and that under no circumstances should alcohol be coupled with all-you-can-eat triple inferno chicken wings. The tempting thing to do at this point is to attribute her decision to free will. She freely chooses to act differently in the future, and it is the force of her will that ensures that she will act differently. Is this the only, or even the best, explanation (E5Preface)? What does it mean if she fails to live up to her resolution? Is it weakness of will, as Aristotle would say, or something else entirely? Spinoza's account does not deny that past events have future effects. In fact, his entire theory rests on following this idea to its absolute conclusion. A very bad hangover may, in fact, be a sufficient cause that results in drinking less. Or it may not. Think of it this way: past causes are like weights on a balance. Some past causes will weigh down one side of the balance; others will weigh down the other side. When the student goes drinking on her birthday, she has some weights on the "don't drink too much" side of the balance. These weights might include past causes such as things her parents told her, things she learned in orientation, or concerns about her safety. Ultimately, however, these weights are outweighed on the "have another drink" side by a desire to celebrate and to have fun with her friends. As a result, the balance tips and she continues drinking. Now, in the throes of her hangover, she has a new weight to add to the "don't drink too much" side. Will it be enough to tip the balance the other way? For Spinoza, this is not something we can predict ahead of time. All we can do is see what happens when she goes out drinking again. If she moderates her drinking, then her past causes were sufficient to determine that outcome. If she ends up drinking too much again, then there is still too much weight on the other side of the balance. Regardless of what happens, though, free will is not required to explain the behavior. Escape from bondage only requires that past causes determine actions in a way that increases rather than decreases power (E5P4 and P5).

Three kinds of knowledge

In the examples of the SUV driver and the drinking student, understanding was the key to escaping bondage. Once I understood why I was cut off, I was no longer angry. Once the student understood her limits, she was less tempted to drink to excess. Spinoza's position here is beginning to sound more and more like Plato's position, where the only real problem is ignorance. There are surely some overlaps. Perhaps we could say it this way: living well arises from understanding well. When the position is stated this way, though, few would disagree with it. In order to fully understand Spinoza's position here, we need to see exactly what understanding is and how it works. Why, precisely, does knowing why the SUV cut me off eliminate my anger? What mechanism is at work here?

There are three kinds of knowledge for Spinoza: imagination, reason, and intuition. Only reason and intuition produce the kind of understanding required to escape bondage. Imagination is "knowledge" that we receive through our senses and through what other people tell us. Spinoza does not really consider imagination knowledge, because it is so often wrong. The real problem with imagination, though (and ultimately the reason why it is often wrong), is that imagination assumes the contingency of things. That is, imagination does not seek the reasons why things are the way they are. Since imagination does not look for the why, it assumes that whatever it knows could be otherwise (E2P40S2).

Reason, in contrast, is real knowledge, and it is real knowledge precisely because it seeks the necessity of things. Reason looks for the necessary connection among modes, among the parts of the universe. It is reason that tells us why the pen lands where it does on the floor. It is reason that understands that, given the identical set of causes, identical effects will result. It is reason that looks for a difference in causes when there is a difference in effects. If an experiment gives two different results, it is reason that painstakingly isolates the variables in an attempt to discover why the effects are different. It is only when we understand why things are the way they are that we have knowledge (E2P40S2).

The third kind of knowledge is intuition. For Spinoza (and philosophers in general), intuition is a way of talking about knowledge that we possess immediately, without deliberation. As we saw above, Aristotle referred to this kind of thinking as "intelligence." For Aristotle, intelligence grasped fundamental principles in the realm of the necessary. There are two important contrasts between Aristotle and Spinoza on this point. First, whereas Aristotle devoted a great deal of time to intellectual virtues that examined contingent objects, Spinoza does not think there are any contingent objects. For Spinoza, everything is necessary, so he would collapse Aristotle's distinction between the practical and theoretical intellect into simply the theoretical intellect. Second, what intuition grasps for Spinoza is not first principles but the relation between the whole and the parts. Regardless of the situation, it is intuition that immediately sees that this could not be otherwise (E2P40S2).

It is often the case, for example, that I do not know the exact connection among things. Not everything is an experiment in which I have control over the variables. But, I *can* always know – regardless of the situation and regardless of its complexity – that it could not have been otherwise. To show how this is the case, let's return to the SUV driver. Finding out why a driver cut me off is actually exceedingly rare. It is much more typical that I never find out why I am cut off. So what if we modify the story? Let's say that I never see the SUV driver turn into the hospital. What can I do then to escape bondage? What I lose if I do not find out why I am cut off is the second kind of knowledge, reason. That is, I do not get to see the necessary connection between this driver, this SUV, the hospital, and me. What I can know, though, in this situation (and in every situation) is that it could not have been otherwise. Why is the driver cutting me off at this intersection? Because this intersection lies between his house and the hospital. Why does he live in this house? Because, given where he works, what was for sale at the time, and the amount he had saved for a down payment, this was his best option. Why does he work here? Because of where he went to college, where he interned, what was available at the time he was looking for a job. Obviously, we can keep asking questions like this. The answers will eventually lead us to the nature of the universe itself. Things are the way they are because everything follows from the necessary causality of the universe as a whole. These kinds of questions also apply to me. Why was I there at that moment to be cut off in the first place? I left a light on, so I went back in the house to turn it off. This delayed my departure by thirty seconds. Why did I leave the light on? My phone rang as I was walking out the door, and I answered it instead of turning off the light. Who called? Why did they call? Why did they call then? Again, no matter which path of causes I follow, I eventually arrive at the nature of the universe itself. For Spinoza, intuition allows us to skip the laborious (and interminable) process of connecting every individual effect to its cause and go straight to the big picture, because the answer is always the same: this could not have been otherwise (E5P27).

It does not matter if the SUV driver cut me off because he was rushing to the hospital. It does not matter if he cut me off because he was late for work. It does not matter if he cut me off because he was not paying attention. It does not even matter if he cut me off intentionally because he is a jerk. None of this matters, because whatever the reason, it could not have been otherwise. To imagine that things could have been otherwise is to imagine a different universe with different laws. Real escape from bondage does not arise when I decide that the SUV driver had a "good" reason for cutting me off (e.g., rushing to the hospital). I am not justified in my anger if I decide that he does not have a "good" reason (e.g., texting). For Spinoza, behind all this talk of "good" reasons lurks the specter of free will. It only makes sense to talk of "good" reasons if one assumes that one could have acted otherwise. There are no "good" or "bad" reasons; there are only reasons, causes that necessarily bring about their effects. For example, the reason that water is wet is neither "good" nor "bad;" it simply, necessarily is. Furthermore, I do not become angry at water's wetness. I accept it. In the same way, to the degree that I can see that being cutting off follows with necessity from an infinite chain of antecedent causes, I will be no more angry with that than I am with water's wetness (E4P50S).

Virtue

In our discussion of Aristotle we spent a lot of time working on the concept of virtue. As we saw, virtue is excellence, but it is an excellence that is specific to what one is doing or thinking. The reason for this concern about virtue is that happiness, or human flourishing, is an activity in accordance with virtue, and flourishing is, of course, the goal of Aristotle's research. In contrast to this, Spinoza spends very little time talking about virtue, but in order to more easily compare Aristotle and Spinoza, let's take a look at what he says about virtue and its relation to the best kind of life.

To begin with, though he does not say this explicitly, Spinoza would agree with Aristotle's claim that happiness is acting in accord with virtue. He would even agree that virtue must involve the exercise of reason. When we turn to Spinoza's definition of "virtue" the differences pile up very quickly. Spinoza writes,

> By *virtue* and *power* I mean the same thing; that is, virtue, insofar as it is related to man, is man's very essence, or nature, insofar as he has power to bring about that which can be understood solely through the laws of his own nature. (E4Def8)

The immediately striking thing about Spinoza's definition is the equation of virtue and power. At first blush this seems very different from Aristotle, who equated virtue and excellence. "Excellence" has numerous moral connotations, while "power" has so many immoral connotations.

Why does Spinoza choose "power" here? The key thing to remember is that we use "power" in two really distinct ways. Many languages keep these two meanings apart by using two different words. Alas, this is not the case in English. Sometimes we use "power" to mean "power over" or "domination." It is from this usage that the immoral connotations of "power" arise. Sometimes we use "power" to mean "power to" or "capability." We see this usage in an exchange such as this: "Will you get the assignment done on time?" "If it's within my power." Here the reference to "power" is a reference to one's abilities and the constraints on them, not domination.

As we saw in the previous chapter, Spinoza is much more interested in the "power to" sense of "power" than the "power over" sense. The question of ethics for Spinoza is not What can I dominate? but What am I capable of? Furthermore, what I am capable of is affected greatly by the way I interact with the world. There are ways of interacting with the world that increase my capabilities, and there are ways of interacting with the world that decrease my capabilities. These interactions are the emotions, and if they decrease my capabilities, I am in bondage. Or, to use Aristotelian language, a decrease in my capabilities is "vice." If the interactions increase my capabilities, that is virtue (E4P38).

It is also precisely at this point that understanding comes back on the scene. If the question of ethics for Spinoza is What am I capable of?, the very next question has to be How do I know what I am capable of? How can I tell the difference between those unvirtuous interactions that decrease my power and those virtuous interactions that increase my power? The answer lies in reason or the understanding. Even more specifically, the answer lies in seeing the necessity of things, the second and third kinds of knowledge. It is only to the degree that I understand myself, the world, and other things that I can know what I am capable of. To the degree that I lack this understanding, my interactions will be confused and result in a decrease in my capabilities (E5P42S).

Freedom

What is hopefully clear by this point is that, even if Spinoza agrees with Aristotle that the best kind of life is a life lived in accord with reason or virtue, the shape of that life well lived is quite different. While Spinoza does speak of "happiness" and even "blessedness" in some cases, the word he most often uses to refer to the best kind of life is "freedom." Wait. What? Freedom? Did Spinoza not argue that freedom is an illusion? Did he not argue that a belief in freedom is the source of most of our problems? No, he argued that *free will* is an illusion and source of most of our problems. Spinoza makes a distinction between freedom and free will. This is difficult for us to countenance, since we so closely associate the two, but freedom is real, while free will is not (E5P42S).

Another philosopher, John Locke, writing a few years after Spinoza's death, illustrates the distinction between freedom and free will very nicely. Suppose, Locke says, that, while you are sleeping, someone transports you in your bed to a room. Upon waking up you discover two things: the one person in the world you most want to talk to and the fact that the only door out of the room is locked. Do you want to talk to this person? If you had been given a choice between talking and not talking to this person, would you choose to talk to this person? Given that it is the person you most want to talk to, the answer to these questions seems to be "yes." Are you free, though? No, you are not free. You are not free because you cannot leave the room. Even though your will is choosing exactly what it wants, you are not free. The conclusion that Locke draws from this thought experiment is that freedom is not a property of the will. Freedom is not a property of the will in the way that roundness is not a property of triangles. It does not make sense to talk about the will being free. Locke concludes that freedom is a claim about power, a claim about one's abilities. Being in a locked room constrains my power, regardless of what my will chooses.[1]

Spinoza would agree that freedom does not apply to the will. The will is determined by past causes, just like everything else in the universe. Spinoza would also agree that freedom is a claim about power. Or, to be precise, freedom and power are synonymous. In fact, the equation of power and freedom completes a long line of interchangeable terms in Spinoza's *Ethics*. There are more, but here are the ones we have discussed:

Living well = Reason/Intuition = Understanding Necessity =
Happiness = Blessedness = Power = Virtue = Freedom

In order to see how this all hangs together, let's return one last time to the SUV driver. He cut me off. I was angry. This anger is bondage. It is bondage because my thoughts and actions are not controlled by me; they are controlled by something that diminishes my abilities. I am not thinking straight. I am not really myself. When I replace

---

[1] John Locke, *Essay Concerning Human Understanding*, Book 2, Chapter 21, §10.

my anger with understanding, though, my power increases. I move from bondage to freedom, not through the will but through power of understanding. Freedom, happiness, the best kind of life is the life lived through understanding. This is a freedom that does not require free will (E5P42S).

There is no question that Spinoza challenges many of our most basic assumptions about human nature and ethics. Spinoza would claim, however, that he is merely being consistent. The biggest casualty of Spinoza's consistency is free will. Ultimately, Spinoza argues that free will is inconsistent with a causally governed universe, and that one need not posit free will in order to give an account of a life well lived. A life well lived arises from understanding the universe and one's place in it, not from imposing one's will in opposition to the order of the universe. For Spinoza, our task is simple to state but difficult to execute: understand yourself, your world, and the things around you well enough that you can combine with what increases your power and avoid what decreases your power. You will not always succeed, but even your failures can be understood; thus you will find "nothing deserving of hatred, derision, or contempt" and you "will endeavor to do well . . . and be glad" (E4P50S).

Summary

Living well depends on the ability to understand that things could not have been otherwise. To waste time and energy supposing that anything could have been different is bondage. Freedom lies in one's ability to act in accord with one's nature.

Questions
1. Is understanding sufficient to overcome bondage?
2. Do you buy the free will/freedom distinction?
3. Does Spinoza's denial of free will lead to apathy rather than freedom?

PART II MORALITY

HOW SHOULD WE ACT?
KANT AND MILL

Morality

The two philosophers that we will read about in this section are Kant and Mill. After Plato and Aristotle, Immanuel Kant (1724–1804) remains one of the most important and influential philosophers in history. Kant is best known for his "critical" philosophy, which seeks a middle path between dogmatism and skepticism. In contrast to Spinoza he argues that humans have free will and that this free will is the key to right action. The key to right action for Kant lies in the intention behind the action, not the consequence of the action.

John Stuart Mill (1806–73) is also influential, particularly in the areas of morality, politics, and probability. Mill was instrumental in the movement to abolish slavery in Great Britain, as well as arguing that women should be given the right to vote. Politically, he was convinced that rights are only defensible to the degree that they are given to everyone. In contrast to Kant, Mill argues that right action is determined by the consequence of the action.

Even though Kant and Mill are directly opposed on the principle of right action, there is a more fundamental way in which they are alike. Both think that the purpose of philosophy is securing "a principle of right action." This task is in marked contrast to Aristotle and Spinoza, who, despite their differences, saw the task of philosophy as living well. In order to highlight this distinction in task, I use the word "ethics" for those philosophies that pursue living well as an end, and I use the word "morality" for those philosophies that use "right action" as an end.

The difference in task between ethics and morality boils down to a difference in the question each is asking. Ethics is asking the question "How should we live?" As we saw, answering this question involves an account of human nature, character, and virtue. Morality is asking the question "How should we act?" Answering this question, as we will see, involves the articulation of principles. Both Kant and Mill agree that the task of philosophy is to answer this question, but they disagree profoundly about the answer.

Thus we find our task doubly complicated. Not only must we decide between competing philosophies, but also we must decide between philosophies that differ in kind, between ethics and morality. It is not that ethics and morality are mutually exclusive, but the question one takes to be primary will color everything that follows.

5

Kant: Happiness is not the Good
(*Groundwork*, Part 1)

Key terms

Good – Good will.
Good will – The intentions behind an action.
Intention – The reason or principle according to which one acts.
Duty – What one *ought* to do. The path to goodness.
Inclination – What one *wants* to do. The path to happiness.
Maxim – A rule for action.

Despite their differences, Spinoza and Aristotle both agree that happiness is the highest good. The equation of happiness and the highest good is precisely what distinguishes ethics from morality. It is precisely because happiness is an activity involving a whole life that its primary focus is on a life well lived. Kant changes that focus. He argues that happiness is not the highest good. As a result, he is much more focused on acting rightly than he is on living well. Part of the difference here is terminological. Kant just defines "happiness" differently from Aristotle and Spinoza. For Kant, as for us, "happiness" simply means "pleasure." There is no suggestion that "happiness" is a way of talking about human flourishing. At this point, we can see another convergence between Kant's position and Aristotle and Spinoza's position. They all agree that pleasure is not the highest good. We can clearly see the difference if we turn the respective positions into formulas:

Aristotle/Spinoza
Good = Happiness ≠ Pleasure

Kant
Good ≠ Happiness = Pleasure

Kant's refusal to identify goodness and happiness opens up possibilities that are unthinkable for Aristotle and Spinoza. For Aristotle and Spinoza, there are only two options: good and happy or bad and unhappy. For Kant there are now four possibilities:

1. Good and Happy
2. Good and Unhappy
3. Bad and Happy
4. Bad and Unhappy

Because there is no necessary connection between goodness and happiness for Kant, it is entirely possible to be good and unhappy or bad and happy. Neither Aristotle nor Spinoza could ask, Would you rather be good or happy? This would be tantamount to asking, Would you rather have water or H_2O to drink? No choice or preference can be given because they are the same thing. Kant's distinction opens up the very possibility of such a choice or preference, except he does not pose it as a matter of preference. He poses it as a moral decision, Is it *better* to be good or happy? Or, given the choice between goodness and happiness, which *ought* I to choose?

To really understand the force of Kant's question, we need to be careful not to mistake it for any other question. The question is not Would I choose my happiness over doing the right thing? The question is not Do people sometimes choose pleasure over goodness? Kant is manifestly not interested in what I do, or even in what most people do. Morality is not decided by majority. Even if most of the people most of the time choose their pleasure over goodness, this does not mean that pursuing pleasure is actually good. No matter what we do, no matter the motivation, we have the capacity to ask, Is this right? Asking this question shows that on some level we know that goodness is morally superior to happiness. Our happiness is only a guide to our pleasure, not a guide to right action. In fact, our happiness can and often does lead us astray with regard to morality. If happiness does not lead to goodness, what does? In answering this question Kant does not stray far from Aristotle and Spinoza. Reason leads to goodness, even in opposition to our happiness. Importantly, though, unlike Spinoza, Kant argues for the existence of free will and claims that our goodness depends on its existence.

Good will is the highest good

Where is reason taking us, though? What is "goodness" for Kant? In order to answer this question he looks at the kinds of things that we call "good." Kant acknowledges that there are all sorts of things we call "good," such as, money, pleasure, intelligence, courage, and the ability to always pick the best thing on the menu at a restaurant. Ultimately, though, all of these goods are only good in a qualified sense. That is, none of these goods is good in itself, but is granted its goodness by something else. Take intelligence, for example. Is intelligence always good, or are there occasions when intelligence produces something bad? Intelligence would allow a bank robber to rob banks better. Intelligence allows a criminal to move from villainy to "cartoonish super-villainy." The same goes for money and pleasure. Both can be used to further good or bad ends. What is behind all these goods that actually makes them good? For Kant, the answer is "good will" (Ak 4:393).[1]

"Good will" is the intention behind one's actions. If the intentions are good, the action is good. This may seem a little surprising, since the much more tempting answer is that the consequences of an action make it bad. For example, the bank robber's intelligence is bad because he uses it to rob banks. The philanthropist's money is good because she uses it to help people. Kant disagrees. Let's try a thought experiment to see why goodness derives from the intention and not the consequence. Let's suppose that Michael Phelps, a swimmer who has won

---

[1] Most Kant texts, including the *Grounding for the Metaphysics of Morals*, are keyed to the critical edition of his work, the *Preussische Akademie* edition. All the citations for Kant in these chapters will indicate this by using "Ak" to refer to the Akademie edition, followed by volume number, then page number. Typically, these page numbers are found in the margins of Kant's text. All quotations in these chapters refer to Kant, *Grounding for the Metaphysics of Morals*, trans. James W. Ellington (Indianapolis: Hackett, 1981).

more Olympic gold medals than anyone, is walking along the beach. He sees someone in the ocean waving his arms and calling for help. Michael leaps into action and swims as quickly as is humanly possible to where he last saw the person. Unfortunately, Michael cannot find him. He has gone. In this case, did Michael use his talent for good? It seems straightforwardly the case that he did, but how can we make that claim? Where exactly is the good here? He did not actually save the person he set out to save. The consequences of this action were plainly bad. Someone died. How can we reconcile the badness of the consequence with the claim to goodness here? It looks as if we have to claim that the goodness lies in the fact that he *tried* to save the drowning person. Somehow, there is moral worth in the attempt, even if it fails. Where exactly, though, do we locate the goodness that makes this particular use of Michael Phelps's swimming talent good? Kant's claim is that the goodness lies in the intention. That is, the fact that Michael was motivated to use his talents to help someone is sufficient for his action to have moral worth, regardless of the outcome. For Kant, moral worth lies in the intention, not in the outcome. It is the intention behind the action, not the consequences of the action, that makes the action good. Furthermore, a will determined to act in this way is good in itself and not dependent on anything else to be good. Thus, good will is the highest good (Ak 4:394).

The practical function of reason

Kant's argument that good will is the highest good puts him at odds with what we have seen of philosophy so far. Unlike Aristotle and Spinoza, Kant severs the necessary connection between goodness and happiness, as well as between reason and happiness. For Aristotle and Spinoza, being reasonable is the very definition of goodness, and acting in accord with reason is the very definition of happiness. Kant is willing to allow that being reasonable is being good, but he in no way guarantees that this will produce happiness.

The first question to ask Kant here is, Why does he not think that reason produces happiness? Kant bluntly states that reason just is not very good at predicting what will make us happy. This is an unpleasant truth that most of us learn at a very young age. I cannot count the number of times that I pestered my parents for a particular toy, or

worse, saved my own money, only to discover that the much-antici-
pated toy was not really that great. Of course, this experience is not
just limited to children choosing toys. It happens all the time. We are
constantly thinking that what we want is going to make us happy, only
to be disappointed on a fairly regular basis (Ak 4:395).

This common experience leads Kant to ask the question If reason
is supposed to produce happiness, then why is it so bad at it? In order
to illustrate what the issue is here, Kant asks us to think about the
way an organism works. An organism works by a kind of division of
labor. The heart pumps blood. The stomach digests food. The lungs
capture oxygen through respiration. Two things follow from this. First,
this division of labor means that each organ is uniquely suited to its
function. Not only does the heart pump blood, but also it does this to
the exclusion of other functions, such as digesting food or capturing
oxygen. Second, and following from the way each organ is suited to its
function, each organ performs its function reliably. We would be in difficult straits if our organs only performed their functions occasionally.
We would quickly die if our hearts only pumped blood 50 percent of
the time. In fact, even if our hearts pumped blood 99 percent of the
time, we would still die. There is thus an exceedingly strong connection between an organ and its function that excludes other functions
and makes the organ perform its function with a high degree of reliabil-
ity. Much to the dismay of our inner ten-year-old, though, reason does
not seem to have a strong connection with happiness. In fact, given
that we often achieve happiness by eschewing reason, it is tempting to
conclude that there is no connection between reason and happiness.
Or, at the very least, to conclude that the purpose of reason is not to
produce happiness (Ak 4:395).

Why can reason not produce happiness? Or, why can reason not
produce happiness reliably? The answer for Kant is simple. Our happiness depends on several series of consequences turning out just
right. Take the hoped-for toy. Not only do I need to fully understand
what it is capable of, but also I need to understand myself well enough
to know whether I will really like it. Beyond that, my happiness will
depend on who else gets the toy. I may like it more if I am the only kid
on the block with one. Or I may be upset, if everyone else gets a similar toy but made by another company. At this point, my happiness is no
longer dependent on me; it is dependent on the whims of advertising,

other children, other children's parents, and the production schedules of multinational corporations. No matter how acute and far-reaching my reason is, it cannot foresee all of these factors and their consequences. Reason cannot produce happiness because happiness is way beyond reason's control. Expecting reason to produce happiness is like expecting the lungs to produce unpolluted air, rather than simply consuming the air that is available. Producing unpolluted air does not lie within the lungs' purview, just as producing happiness does not lie within reason's purview (Ak 4:396).

The idea that most consequences are beyond our control is a theme that runs throughout Kant's moral theory. His response to this is not to develop a more subtle reason capable of predicting the consequences with greater accuracy. His response is to argue that reason must have some other purpose than predicting consequences. Obviously, reason's purpose would have to be something that it has some measure of control over, and something that it can produce reliably. Not surprisingly, the only thing that fits the bill here for Kant is good will. That is, though we cannot have control over the *consequences* of our actions, we can have control over the *intentions* behind our actions. As we saw in the example above, Michael Phelps has no control over whether the person he is trying to save drowns before he gets there. What he does have control over is his intention to save the person drowning. This is where moral worth lies. This is what reason has control over, and this control is the proper function of reason (Ak 4:396).

The two motivations for action

Unfortunately, reason is not the only force vying for control of our actions. All philosophers note that we are not always reasonable. If we were, there would be no need for philosophy. As we have seen, different philosophers place the blame for our unreasonable actions in different places, whether it be ignorance, weakness of will, or bondage to causes opposed to our nature. For Kant, the source of our unreasonable actions is what he calls "inclination." Inclination is what we want to do. Our inclinations are, for the most part, determined by pleasure. That is, Kant recognizes, just as Aristotle does, that everyone wants to be happy. Also, just as Aristotle claims, most people think happiness is pleasure. The major difference here is that Kant accepts this equation, while Aristotle denies it, though both admit that pleasure is a principal motivation for all people.

Reason and pleasure, these are the two great motivations for action. We already know that reason's purpose is not to produce pleasure, but what does it produce? Or what do we call it when reason controls intention? Kant calls the alignment of intention with reason "duty." Duty is what we *ought* to do, while inclination is what we *want* to do. Notice that this is another way of stating the distinction between being good and being happy. Doing our duty is good, while we presume that following our inclinations will lead to happiness. As Kant never tires of pointing out, though, following our inclinations does not always lead to happiness. With this opposition in mind, one of the ways we can think about Kant's moral theory is trading in the uncertainty of happiness for the certainty of goodness. Regardless of whether we are happy, we can always be good (Ak 4:397).

Because duty and inclination are distinct, there are four ways that they can relate to one another. Or, for any given action, there are four possible combinations of duty and inclination that motivate it. Thus, actions may be motivated:

1. In opposition to duty and from inclination
2. In accord with duty and from a mediate inclination
3. In accord with duty and from an immediate inclination
4. From duty and without inclination.

In the first case, Kant has in mind the kinds of things most people have in mind when they think of immoral acts: lying, cheating, stealing, killing. We can see, here, that Kant's answer to the problem of why people do bad things lies in the motivation. That is, there are times when our concern with pleasure (or the avoidance of pain) is so great that it overwhelms any motivation arising from duty (Ak 4:397).

The next two cases turn on the distinction between mediate and immediate inclination and are a little difficult to sort out. Let's imagine a shopkeeper faced with two different scenarios. In the first scenario, a little boy comes into the store. The shopkeeper has seen him before and is convinced that he has stolen candy from the shop. This time, however, the boy comes to the counter with some candy and empties his pockets full of change onto the counter. There is a great deal more money on the counter than the candy is worth. The shopkeeper is tempted to take all of it to make up for what the boy has stolen. He does not, though. He takes only what the candy is worth. His reasoning is simple. It would be very bad for business if someone discovered that he was cheating little kids out of their money. In this case, the shopkeeper does the right thing. That is, his actions are in accord with duty. However, his real motivation for doing the right thing is not the pleasure that he would immediately receive from running his shop in an orderly fashion. No, his real motivation does not lie in the pleasure of the immediate act, but in the avoidance of future pain. The possible consequences of cheating a child are bad enough to motivate his good behavior here. This is what Kant means by "mediate inclination." In contrast to this, an immediate inclination motivates through the pleasure of the act itself. Suppose this same shopkeeper really liked making change and really liked doing it well. In this case, the shopkeeper's motivation for not cheating the child is the pleasure he receives from making change correctly. Here he happens to do the right thing because it accords with his immediate pleasure (Ak 4:398).

In the last case, notice the shift in Kant's vocabulary. He goes from "in accord with duty" to "from duty." Quite a lot is at stake in this shift. Part of the distinction hinges on a possibility that philosophers have always been aware of. It is possible to do the right thing for the wrong reason. That is, everyone would agree that the actions of the shopkeeper in cases two and three were correct, even though the reasons behind those actions were suspect. All right actions done with suspect motivation are, for Kant, merely in accord with duty. He reserves the phrase "from duty" solely for those right actions that are done for the right reasons. In this case, the shopkeeper's actions would only be from duty if his only motivation for dealing fairly with the boy was that it was the right thing to do without regard for his immediate or future happiness (Ak 4:398).

Kant's position here puts him in a bit of a bind. To begin with, it puts him at odds with Aristotle, who claimed that one does not possess virtue without taking pleasure in it. That is, if I acted excellently without taking pleasure in it, I have not really acted excellently. In Kant's defense, the real issue here is motivation. Kant is saying that if I am doing the act *for* the pleasure, then it is not morally worthwhile.

This raises a second difficulty for Kant, though. In this case it looks as if the only way I can act from duty is if I do not enjoy it. Only then can I really be sure that my inclinations are kept at bay.

This just seems like a really awful way to live. Should I only do things I do not like in order to ensure that my motivations are pure? Thankfully, for Kant the answer is "No." Kant's purpose here is not to suck all the pleasure out of our lives, but to show the limits of a morality based on external actions. Recall how dependent Aristotle's ethics was on which actions would be praised or blamed. Kant deftly points out that actions that many would find praiseworthy might be done for the wrong reasons. Externally, there is no way to tell the difference between actions in accord with duty and actions from duty. What we really need is a way of determining our duty that is not dependent on the praise of others, that depends on an internal principle, not external validation. Only then can we ensure that goodness rather than happiness is our motivation (Ak 4:399).

Three propositions of morality

Before moving on to how we might determine our duty in the Second Section, Kant concludes the First Section of the *Groundwork* with three propositions that he has gleaned from an examination of the difference between being good and being happy:

1. An action must be done from duty in order to have moral worth.
2. Moral worth lies in the maxim, not the consequence.
3. Duty arises from respect for the law.

The first proposition should come as no surprise. Most of what Kant has been saying up to this point supports this claim. It is better to be good than happy. Only right actions done for the right reason are morally worthwhile. Both of these are encapsulated in Kant's very precise phrase "from duty" (Ak 4:399–400).

The next two propositions will require some work because they introduce new vocabulary and new concepts. In proposition two, Kant introduces the notion of "maxim." It is not a word we use very much today, and if we do it is equivalent to "saying" or "proverb." Kant does not mean it that way at all, though. A "maxim" for Kant is "a rule we live by." Now, we live by all sorts of rules. A quick look back on my day shows that I always have Raisin Bran and tea for breakfast and that I always have milk and sugar in my tea. This is a rule that I live by, a rule by which I determine my actions: in this case, breakfast-related actions. Much like habits in Aristotle, maxims in Kant determine a wide range of our actions. We are rule-governed creatures for Kant, and the key to morality lies in determining whether those maxims are motivated by goodness or happiness (Ak 4:400).

Once we know that a maxim is a rule that we live by, the rest of the proposition comes into focus. Kant's claim here harkens back to the opening lines of the *Groundwork*. Goodness lies in the intention not in the consequence. Michael Phelps's action is morally worthwhile, regardless of whether he saves the drowning person or not. The moral worth lies in the rule he lives by – the maxim, not in whether he is able to actually accomplish his purpose. "Save drowning people" is a morally worthwhile rule, even if no one is saved. Furthermore, as we have also seen, the consequences are unpredictable and out of our control. Kant is unwilling to locate moral worth here because moral worth would have more to do with luck than reason. Consequences can only tell us how much pleasure or pain has been produced. They cannot tell us anything about the character of the person who produced them (Ak 4:400).

The third proposition is the most difficult because it introduces two new ideas, "respect" and "law." We can clear up respect pretty quickly, if we think about situations in which we show respect. For example, I notice that when I get up in front of a classroom, the students are generally respectful. They are quiet. They pay attention. Most put away their phones, and those who do not try to be discreet about it. I take it that the respect shown here is a function of my being in front of the classroom, rather than respect for me personally. Students give this same level of respect to their peers when their peers are presenting in front of the class. What exactly is the respect doing, though? This becomes clear if we return to the duty/inclination opposition. Do the students want to put away their phones, take notes, and listen carefully to what I am saying? No, they would probably much rather be interacting with friends either in the class or on social media. That is, their desire for pleasure *inclines* them away from paying attention. Most students overcome these inclinations, though, to pay attention and do what is right. Kant would say that it is respect that allows us to overcome our inclinations and do our duty (Ak 4:400).

Law is a little more difficult, but it is worth getting straight, since it will play an important role in Kant's philosophy going forward. To begin with, Kant is not concerned about any particular law, such as "Do not steal." He is not concerned about any particular law because that would prevent him from talking about duty as such. He could only talk about the duty to a particular law: the duty not to steal, for example. So, in order to talk about duty as such, Kant needs to talk about law as such. What does this mean? How can Kant talk about "law as such"? In order to do this, Kant needs to distinguish between form and content. Particular laws are particular by having different content. What makes all particular laws a law in the first place, though, is that they all have a common form, the form of law. Thus, by the "form of law," Kant means "lawlikeness" or "lawfulness" (Ak 4:401–2)

What sets lawlike things apart from non-lawlike things is a particular kind of relationship, a necessary relationship. That is, lawlike things propose a necessary relationship. In the case of conceptual and mathematical relationships, this is easy to see. There is a necessary relationship between the concept of a mountain and the concept of a valley. It is impossible to think of a mountain without also thinking of a valley. In the same way, it is impossible to think of a triangle without also thinking that its interior angles add up to 180 degrees. There is a lawlike relation among the components of these concepts. In the same way, there is a lawlike relation that exists between an intention and its action. In philosophy, this relation takes the form of an "ought." Even though I might be inclined to steal, even though I might see some pleasure or advantage in stealing, I ought not steal. This is my duty, and it arises out of respect for the ought, which is the form that lawlikeness takes in morality (Ak 4:401–2).

The discovery of our duty in any particular situation hinges on uncovering the particular ought that governs the relation between intention and action. What Kant needs, then, is a test for our intentions, our maxims, to see if they live up to the standard of the ought. This is precisely where Kant turns in the next section of the *Groundwork*. He calls this test "the categorical imperative."

Summary

Given a choice between being good and being happy, Kant argues that only being good is morally worthwhile. Being good is a question of acting according to our duty, which means our actions take the form of "lawlikeness." We act rightly, morally, when duty rather than inclination is the source of our actions.

Questions

1. Is Kant right about the distinction between goodness and happiness?
2. Does goodness lie in the intention rather than the consequences?
3. How can we know what our intentions are?

6

Kant: The Categorical Imperative
(*Groundwork*, Part 2)

Key terms

Will – The faculty that creates and follows laws/imperatives.
Hypothetical imperative – Laws that seek an end outside themselves (if X, then Y).
Categorical imperative – Laws that are their own end (X, because X is right).
Autonomy – Self-ruling.
Heteronomy – Being ruled by others.

Kant has a problem. This is not just his problem. He thinks it is a problem with philosophy in general. The problem is with certainty. How can we be certain that we have done our duty? In Aristotle, this problem was solved pretty easily. I know I have done the right thing when I am praised for my actions. Ideally, this praise would reinforce the behavior and it would become a fixed part of my character. This, for Aristotle, is the path to human flourishing. Kant points out, though, that praise only gets me so far. Praise only tells me that my actions are *in accord with* duty. Praise can never tell me if my actions are *from* duty. As we saw, whether my actions are from duty is dependent on my maxim, the rule I am acting on. Other people cannot see the principle; they can only see the action. I am the only person that can know the maxim I am acting on. Is this enough, though? Is it possible I could deceive myself about the real reasons for my action? Obviously. So, what is a philosopher to do? Where is certainty going to come from? The short answer is the categorical imperative, but understanding why this is the case will require some explanation.

Avoiding skepticism and dogmatism

In this section of the *Groundwork*, Kant draws heavily from his other works in philosophy, particularly his *Critique of Pure Reason*. Importantly, one of the concerns animating that work is also certainty, but certainty about knowledge rather than action. From Kant's perspective, the philosophers that preceded him were either too certain (dogmatic) or not certain enough (skeptical). This certainty (or lack thereof) arises from taking different models for knowledge. The dogmatic philosophers take mathematics for their model and think that all knowledge could achieve that level of certainty. The skeptical philosophers take the natural sciences for their model, which means that knowledge claims are always revisable in the face of new evidence. On this model, knowledge only possesses degrees of probability, never mathematical certainty. Kant's philosophy seeks a middle path between these two extremes that he calls "critical philosophy."

The chief feature of Kant's critical philosophy is that while he recognizes the truth of both positions, he does not simply combine them. Rather, he uses a strategy that we saw in our discussion of Aristotle, the form/content distinction. He thinks that the mathematical, deductive model of certainty employed by dogmatic philosophers is the best way to think about the *form* of our knowledge, while the inductive, experimental model of the skeptical philosophers is the best way to think about the *content* of our knowledge. Thus, even though we always find form and content together, it is, in principle, possible to separate them.[1]

From the standpoint of philosophy, Kant's move here is really important. He thinks that fully following the skeptical philosophy leads to an inability to know what our duty is. We could never be certain about our duty because it would always be subject to revision. At the same time, following the dogmatic philosophy leads to a kind of fanaticism that would allow other people to determine our duty for us. By steering a path between relativism and fanaticism, Kant thinks we can determine our duty with certainty. This path is made possible by

---

[1] Kant, *Critique of Pure Reason* (B1–2). References to the *Critique of Pure Reason* typically do not follow the Akadamie numbering system. Instead, they use an A/B numbering system that refers to the first/second editions of the work.

sharply distinguishing between the form and content, even if they work together in practice. What we will see is that the categorical imperative works by separating out the form and testing the form in isolation from its content, because certainty lies with the form (Ak 4:408).

The will

Similarly to Aristotle, Kant makes a distinction between the practical and the theoretical uses of reason. Unlike Aristotle, the difference between the two in Kant is that the theoretical use of reason concerns knowledge, while the practical use of reason concerns action. Because the practical use of reason concerns action, it is synonymous with "will" for Kant. Will is the unique capacity that rational creatures have that allows them to create and follow laws they set for themselves. Unlike in Spinoza, the will is free, but (and this should sound familiar by now) only insofar as it acts according to reason. That is, there are two motivations for the will, duty and inclination. Will that chooses according to inclination is unfree. Will that chooses according to duty is free (Ak 4:412–13).

How exactly does the will work, though? For Kant, the will works by creating and following laws, which he calls "imperatives." There are two basic kinds of imperative, "hypothetical" and "categorical." The difference between these two kinds of imperative lies in whether the imperative has an additional goal beyond it (hypothetical), or whether it can be fulfilled simply by following it (categorical). This is kind of a strange way to think about rules, but let's see if we can illustrate what is at stake. I mentioned above that one of the rules I live by (maxim) is that I have Raisin Bran and tea for breakfast every morning. What kind of rule is this, hypothetical or categorical? Am I following this rule for its own sake, or am I trying to achieve some other goal by following this rule? I am clearly trying to achieve something else here. When I wake up, I am hungry. Following this rule sates my hunger. Eating breakfast also gives me sufficient energy to accomplish my morning tasks. Without my breakfast (especially the tea), I would become extraordinarily cranky before the morning ended. This rule is manifestly a hypothetical imperative (Ak 4:414–15).

What about categorical imperatives? What sort of rules do we follow for their own sake? When I was younger, I would dash out of the house yelling, "Bye, Mom, I'm going out to play!" Just before the door slammed shut behind me, I could hear her say, "Be good!" It is clearly an imperative, but what kind of imperative is it? Did my mom want me to be good to achieve some other goal, or is being good an end in itself? Whatever I may have thought of it (if I thought of it at all), my mom surely intended it to be a categorical imperative. Being good was not the path to another goal, as eating breakfast was. Being good was a rule to be followed for its own sake. Kant thinks that many of our moral rules are categorical. Do not lie. Do not cheat. Do not steal. Do not kill. These are all rules that we follow for their own sake, because they are the right thing to do, not because they lead to something else. Obviously, even categorical imperatives can be perverted. I might be on my best behavior as Christmas approaches in the hopes of getting more presents (or, at least, getting fewer taken away). In this case, I have turned the categorical imperative "be good" into the hypothetical imperative "if I'm good, then I'll get more presents." The important point for Kant is that categorical imperatives are possible, and if they are possible, that is where moral worth lies (Ak 4:416).

First formulation of the categorical imperative

The categorical imperative, then, tests the rules we live by to see what kind of rules they are. Are they rules we are following to achieve something else, or are they rules we are following for their own sake? If it turns out the rules (maxims) are hypothetical, then there is no moral worth in following them and it is our duty to do the opposite. If it turns out that the maxims are categorical, then there is moral worth in following them and we have discovered our duty. Thus, putting our maxims to the test reveals our duty, whether they pass or fail. Kant formulates the categorical imperative in three ways. The first formulation he calls the "universal law" or "law of nature" formulation, and it reads, "act only according to that maxim whereby you can at the same time will that it should become a universal law" (Ak 4:421). In order to show how this formulation of the categorical imperative works, Kant tests four different maxims. All the maxims fail, but it is crucially important to see why they fail in order to understand Kant's position. Kant's choice of the four examples corresponds to four kinds of duty that can be organized in a simple table:

Four kinds of duty	Duty to self	Duty to others
Perfect duties	Example 1: Is a duty to suicide possible? No.	Example 2: Is a duty to make lying promises possible? No.
Imperfect duties	Example 3: Can I will a duty to laziness? No.	Example 4: Can I will a duty to be uncharitable? No.

In the first example, Kant imagines a man so beaten down by misfortune that he considers suicide. Is this his duty? In order to figure this out, the first thing we need to do is see what maxim is operative here. The maxim, in this case, goes something like this: In order to avoid the future pain that may be caused by living, it is better to end my life now. Now, there is no question that suicide will bring and end to pain and suffering, but remember that that is not the goal for Kant. The goal for Kant is goodness, which is entirely distinct from questions of pleasure and pain. Kant can freely admit that pain might be diminished by this act, but he has no interest in calculating how much pain is reduced or how much pleasure is increased. These are not moral concerns for Kant. How can we figure out whether it is actually good to act on this maxim? For Kant, we must look at the form of the maxim to see whether the form achieves what we called, in the last chapter, "lawlikeness," and here Kant calls "a universal law of nature" (Ak 4:422).

By "law of nature," Kant has something like an instinct in mind: that is, something that we do automatically, like birds flying South for the winter. Kant is asking us to try to imagine the suicidal man's maxim as an instinct that would be implanted in everyone. That is, what if everyone automatically committed suicide, when life promised more pain than pleasure? Here we must use the greatest caution, lest we misread Kant. The tempting answer is to say, "Everyone would commit suicide, and humans would cease to exist. Therefore, don't commit suicide." *But, this is manifestly, absolutely NOT what Kant is saying.* Let's take a moment to figure out why. Why does Kant's argument not hinge on the possibility of everyone committing suicide? Because, these are *CONSEQUENCES*. Remember, moral worth lies in the maxim, not the consequences. The categorical imperative is not a test for consequences. It is not asking us to imagine a world where everyone does X, and then wonders whether the world would be a better or worse place. Many people read Kant this way, but it is, in fact, a much better summary of our next philosopher, Mill, than it is of Kant (Ak 4:422).

If the suicidal man's maxim does not fail because the consequences are bad, why does it fail? Let's return to the idea of instinct from above. Kant says that such an instinct would contradict itself. The first thing we need to get clear on is what "contradiction" means in philosophy. It is a technical term that means more than simple disagreement. It means that something can be both A and not-A at the same time. A square circle, for example, is a contradiction. That is, it claims to be both a circle and not a circle at the same time. The issue with contradictions is not that they have bad consequences, but that they are unthinkable. I cannot even imagine a square circle. The other important aspect to contradictions that Kant is exploiting here is that they are a problem with the form rather than a problem with the content. That is, a contradiction can be seen simply by looking at the claim without reference to the consequences. That is how Kant zeroes in on the form in the categorical imperative. It is crucial to ask with regard to this formulation of the categorical imperative, Where does the contradiction lie?

Where does the contradiction lie in the suicidal man's maxim? What is impossible about the rule he lives by? Why could such a rule not be implanted as an instinct? Let's look carefully at what the rule claims. The desire to pursue pleasure and avoid pain is essential to the furtherance of life. Without this desire we would quickly lose our motivation to do anything. The suicidal man's maxim, however, turns this desire against itself. He is trying to further life by destroying it. The problem here is not that the maxim produces bad consequences but that it is self-contradictory. Trying to implant this maxim as an instinct would be like trying to implant an instinct in birds to fly North *and* South for the winter. Again, the problem is not that such an instinct would have bad consequences; it is that such an instinct cannot even be conceived in the first place. As a result of this contradiction, it is the man's duty not to commit suicide (Ak 4:422).

The second example involves a man who needs a loan but can only get the money if he lies about whether he will be able to repay it. His maxim goes something like this: Though I normally tell the truth, it is OK to lie when I am really in need. Once again, Kant freely admits that the consequences of such a lie might work out very well for this man. He gets the money; he gets out of difficulty and lives happily every after. As always, though, the question for Kant is not whether an action increases happiness, but whether it is right. So, let's test this maxim not for its possible consequences, but to see if its form is consistent with itself. Kant says that once we attempt to think this maxim as a universal law, it fails to achieve lawlikeness. It cannot be a universal law because its form is self-contradictory. Lying only works against the background of truth-telling. That is, lying is dependent on its opposition to the truth. This maxim obliterates that distinction and tries to imagine a world where every statement is both true and false at the same time. Formally, this is no different from an instinct that keeps you alive by killing you. Again, the problem is not the consequences; it is that such a maxim is unthinkable as a law (Ak 4:422).

In the third and fourth examples, Kant shifts gears from perfect to imperfect duty. A perfect duty is one that admits of no exceptions, while an imperfect duty allows for some leeway in terms of how it is pursued. The importance of this shift lies in the way that maxims are analyzed. As we saw, in the first two examples, the maxims failed because they were self-contradictory. In the last two examples, about developing one's talents and about being charitable, the locus of contradiction moves. The last two maxims fail because no rational creature would will such a thing. Thus, these examples hinge on what can be rationally willed (Ak 4:422).

In the third example, a man wonders whether he should develop his talents or give in to laziness. Kant says right away that there is no contradiction in imagining such a maxim as everyone's instinct. Such a world is thinkable. Furthermore, Kant is certain that such a world might be a happier, more pleasant world. But, none of this tells us whether it is right. Kant thinks such a man is duty-bound to develop his talents. His reasoning is that rational creatures will the development of their abilities, because these abilities can be helpful in all sorts of ways. Admittedly, this sounds very much as if Kant is arguing based on the consequences, but let's try a thought experiment. Is it possible to imagine a world where people do not use their left arms? Yes. Can we imagine that this right-arm-only world is happier? That is a little weird but it is not impossible. Would we will a world where people voluntarily give up the use of their left arms? No. Even if it would make everyone happier? Still no. Why? We have no idea what we might use our left arm for. It would be irrational to give up such a capacity. For Kant, the problem here is that there is a flaw in the willing. It is not contradictory *per se*, but no one would will such a thing. Thus, this man has a duty to develop his talents, but he has some leeway with regard to how and when he develops them (Ak 4:423).

In the fourth example, a man of means decides that he would rather not help others. Just as in the previous example, Kant says that not only can we imagine a world where everyone acts this way, but also that such a world would be preferable to the current hypocritical one in which people spout high-minded platitudes about benevolence but also cheat and steal from their neighbors. So, again, the issue is neither conceivability nor consequences. The issue, as in the last case, is whether or not a rational creature would will such a maxim as universal law. Kant thinks no rational creature would will such a thing, and the reasons closely parallel developing one's talents. The difference here is that instead of being concerned with one's own abilities, the concern is with one's relationship to others. We would no more will to stop using our left arms than we would will to give up all relationships to other people. We would not cut ourselves off, even if we knew it might make us happier in the long run. It would simply be irrational. Thus, this man has a duty to help others, though he can choose the time and manner in which he does it (Ak 4:423).

Second formulation of the categorical imperative

In some ways it is unfortunate that Kant leads with the universal law formulation of the categorical imperative. Not only is it more difficult to understand than the other two formulations, but also people usually start there since it is first. As a result, people quickly become confused or misconstrue Kant's position. The second formulation, known as the "end-in-itself" formulation, is much more straightforward. While it is still a test for maxims, it does not depend on finding a contradiction either in the form of the maxim or in the possibility of willing it. Rather, it depends on a distinction between maxims that treat people as ends-in-themselves and maxims that treat people merely as means to something else. This distinction nicely parallels the one we have already seen between categorical and hypothetical imperatives (Ak 4:428).

As we saw above, Kant divides duties into duties directed at oneself and duties directed toward others. This formulation of the categorical imperative supposes that there are two basic ways to treat self and others. Either we treat them merely as a means to some other end, or we treat them as an end-in-themselves. Treating people merely as a means is to use them to further our own ends. Let's suppose that I volunteer at an orphanage. I spend three evenings a week helping children. Now let's also suppose that the only reason that I volunteer at the orphanage is that I thought it would look really great on my online dating profile and that I would get more dates this way. In this instance, even though the orphans are being helped, I am still using them merely as a means. My actions do not treat them as ends-in-themselves but as tools to burnish my image. Treating the orphans as an end-in-themselves would mean helping them simply because it is the right thing to do. For Kant, there is only moral worth in those maxims that treat people as ends rather than means (Ak 4:429).

With this new formulation in mind, Kant returns to the same four examples that we looked at above. We can go through them much more quickly this time, though. The suicidal man should not commit suicide, because he would be treating himself merely as a means to the cessation of pain. The poor man should not make a lying promise, because he would be treating the lender merely as a means to acquire money. The lazy man should develop his talents, because, in failing to do so, he fails to treat himself as an end-in-itself. The stingy man should be charitable, because he too fails to treat others as ends-in-themselves (Ak 4:429–30).

Again, notice the shift that occurs between the perfect and imperfect duties. For the perfect duties, the failed maxim actively treats someone merely as a means. For the imperfect duties, no one is treated as a means; it is just that the maxim fails to live up to the standard of duty. The first two failures are sins of commission. The actor did wrong. The second two failures are sins of omission. The actor failed to do right.

Third formulation of the categorical imperative

The third formulation of the categorical imperative is called the "autonomy" formulation. "Autonomy" means "self-governing." I am autonomous when I give the law to myself. We usually see the word "autonomy" in a political context to talk about whether a country is capable of ruling itself. Kant uses it here in a moral context to flesh out the implications of his theory. The idea is that morality is inseparable from my ability to govern myself. Stated this way, it is difficult to see how Kant differs from other philosophers. Everyone we have read is adamant that self-control is one of the key components to living well. Kant, however, is not simply talking about self-control. His position is much more radical.

In order to see the radicality of Kant's position, it will be helpful to see what he opposes to "autonomy." The opposite of autonomy for Kant is not something like recklessness; it is what he calls "heteronomy." "Heteronomy" means "governed by others." The crux of the opposition lies in the source of governance. Either maxims are in accord with reason (as determined by the test of the categorical imperative) and thus one's duty, or maxims are not in accord with reason and thus opposed to duty. When we act from duty, we give ourselves the law and are thus autonomous. When we act merely in accord with duty (or in opposition to it), the laws governing our actions come from elsewhere and are thus heteronomous. As we have seen, as rational creatures we are capable of creating and following the laws we live by. Kant's focus here is the source of those laws. Either the law springs from reason internally, and we are autonomous, or the law springs from inclination externally, and its source is heteronomous (Ak 4:440–1).

The autonomy/heteronomy distinction maps directly onto the other distinctions that we have seen throughout our discussion of Kant: goodness/happiness, intention/consequence, duty/inclination, certainty/uncertainty, end-in-itself/merely a means, etc. With this in mind, we can return briefly to Kant's four examples to show that the results are the same. The suicidal man is violating his autonomy by killing himself. The poor man is violating the autonomy of the lender by lying. Both the lazy man and the uncharitable man fail to live up to either the autonomy of self or the autonomy of others. The conclusion to Kant's analysis of autonomy is that I am responsible for determining the moral law for myself and only myself. Any other source of the moral law is heteronomous and thus fails to live up to duty. My parents cannot determine my morality. Society cannot determine my morality. Religion cannot determine my morality. It is solely my responsibility. Anything else is heteronomy (Ak 4:431).

The kingdom of ends

It would be easy to assume that with the autonomy formulation, Kant has fallen into the kind of skepticism and relativism that he was trying to avoid. How does the requirement for autonomy avoid the charge of relativism? As we have seen, this is a recurring problem. How do we acknowledge that people are different without claiming that individual moralities are different? The answer for Kant (as it was for Aristotle) is reason. People are different, but reason is the same everywhere. Everyone is subject to the same formal constraints of reason. No one anywhere can conceive of a square circle. Thus, even though the responsibility for determining one's duty lies with the individual, everyone takes the same test, and the results will not conflict. Kant thinks it is impossible that two people testing similar maxims will get opposed results, because reason remains the consistent standard in both tests.

The result of everyone both legislating and following the moral law individually under the overarching unity of reason would be what Kant calls "a kingdom of ends." In the kingdom of ends, everyone is both a king and a subject. Everyone is a king because each determines what the law is individually. Everyone is a subject because each is subject to those individual laws. In such a kingdom, the dignity of every person would be recognized as worthwhile for its own sake. The safeguarding of everyone's dignity would arise from the fact that everyone would treat both self and others as ends and never merely as means (Ak 4:433).

Kant's beautiful vision of everyone living in harmony by following the moral law follows from the very simple question with which we began, Is it better to be good or happy? For Kant, it is better to be good, and goodness lies in the intention, not the consequence. The way in which we know our intentions are good is by testing them by the categorical imperative. The test of the categorical imperative tells us whether the maxim seeks only the good, or seeks some kind of happiness. If the maxim seeks only the good, it is our duty. Only I can determine my duty for myself, but if we each seek our own duty, the result will be a kingdom of ends where everyone's dignity is respected.

Summary

Right action depends on ensuring that the will conforms to reason. Kant calls the test for this conformity the categorical imperative. Although Kant provides three formulations of the categorical imperative, they each test whether our maxims are thinkable or willable. Those that are, are our duty.

Questions

1. Are actions in conformity with reason *always* moral?
2. Can we be certain about the rightness of our actions?
3. Does the categorical imperative guarantee this certainty?

7

Mill: Happiness is Pleasure
(*Utilitarianism*, Chapters 1 and 2)

Key terms

Principle of utility – Actions are right to the degree that they produce the greatest happiness for the greatest number.

General law – Statistical likelihood. What is the case for most of the people most of the time.

Universal law – Necessity. What is the case without exception.

Pleasure – There are two basics types: high and low. High pleasures are pleasures of the mind. Low pleasures are pleasures of the body.

Mill is baffled by all the confusion surrounding morality. He cannot believe that, after two millennia of debate, no explicit consensus about the *summum bonum*, or highest good, has arisen. This lack of explicit consensus is especially disconcerting because Mill thinks that *implicitly* everyone really agrees about the highest good. Not only does everyone agree that happiness is the highest good, despite what Kant may have argued, but also everyone agrees that happiness is pleasure. Here Mill aligns himself with a tradition that has its roots in the ancient philosophy of Epicurus, but runs counter to everything we have seen here. Furthermore, though Mill's concern about the highest good seems more allied with the ethical concern of Aristotle and Spinoza, ultimately, Mill's philosophy is trying to answer the same kind of moral question that Kant is: namely, How should we act? Mill's answer to this question is appealingly intuitive. Actions are right, morally worthwhile, our duty, to the degree that they produce pleasure. Given a choice

between two possible courses of action, the right course of action is
the one that produces the greatest pleasure for the greatest number.
Mill calls this principle of right action "the principle of utility," and thus
names his philosophy "utilitarianism."

In order to highlight Mill's differences from the other philosophers
we have looked at, let's add Mill to the formulas from previous chapters:

Aristotle/Spinoza
Good = Happiness ≠ Pleasure

Kant
Good ≠ Happiness = Pleasure

Mill
Good = Happiness = Pleasure

We can see clearly that Aristotle, Spinoza, and Kant all depend on a
refusal to equate "goodness" and "pleasure." None of them thinks that
pleasure is wholly bad, only that pleasure's goodness depends on something else. In contrast to this, Mill simply and straightforwardly identifies
goodness and pleasure. While Mill's move here has the great advantage
of clarifying philosophy immensely, it is not without its difficulties. The
biggest difficulty in making pleasure and goodness synonymous is that
there are times when pursuing pleasure is obviously wrong. If, for example, I see someone trapped in a burning building and decide that it would
be more pleasurable to eat ice cream than help, this is surely a case
where pleasure has led me astray. At this point, Kant can simply say that
being good is better than being happy. Aristotle and Spinoza can say that
pleasure and the good are not equivalent. Neither of these routes is
available to Mill, though. He must walk the difficult path of arguing that,
while all pleasure is good, some pleasures are better than others, and
that morality consists in pursuing the best kind of pleasure.

Morality is a principle

In order to see how Mill arrives at the equation of goodness,
happiness, and pleasure, let's follow his argument from the beginning.
The problem with philosophy up to this point is that it has failed to

identify a universally agreed-upon principle that allows one to distinguish between right and wrong. Mill seeks to rectify this failure by providing such a principle. His argument proceeds by process of elimination. He proposes objections and alternative theories. When all of these are eliminated, Mill's theory is the last one standing (9).[1]

The first and most obvious objection is that morality does not require a principle. There are many instances in science and mathematics where principles are the result of research rather than its ground. Take Darwin's theory of natural selection, for example. Darwin spent years carefully observing the diversity of species before proposing the theory that species are not natural kinds but arise through "descent with modification." In fact, Darwin's theory led him away from the principle that had hitherto dominated biology: namely, that species pre-exist individuals and are unchanging. Perhaps, Mill ponders, morality is like biology in this respect. Maybe we have not figured out the principle of morality because it will be the result of our continued research rather than its starting point. Mill, however, quickly dismisses this possibility, because there is a crucial difference between morality and science. Morality, he reasons, is a theory of action. A theory of action requires a goal. That goal must be known beforehand, or the action itself becomes random. I must know *why* I am doing something before I do it; otherwise, my action has no meaning. Furthermore, I must have a means to achieving this goal. For Mill, the means to achieving the goal of action must be some kind of principle. It must be a principle because it requires judgment and discernment (10).

There are those who would argue, though, that the means to achieving one's goal is instinctive rather than principled. By "instinctive" Mill means arriving at moral judgments through a kind of sensation, that we would "see" the rightness of an action in the same way that we see the redness of an apple. Mill has two problems with this view. The first problem is that moral judgments do not seem to work this way. We do not really "judge" something to be red; we simply acknowledge that it is, in fact, red. Seeing is always a particular and widely varied experience, but judgments of right and wrong are much

---

[1] While there is a Standard Edition of Mill's works, other editions of his works are not keyed to it. As a result, I will refer to the page numbers of a widely available (and affordable) edition, John Stuart Mill, *Utilitarianism* (Buffalo: Prometheus, 1987).

more general. The second problem, and this follows from the first, is that insofar as a judgment is being offered, reason, not sensation, must be the source of the judgment. This brings us back to Mill's initial claim that there must be a principle involved (11).

What kind of principle, though? Mill offers two alternatives, intuitive and inductive. These two alternatives precisely delineate the difference that Mill sees between his philosophy and Kant's. Kant's moral theory is intuitive, while Mill's is inductive. For Mill, what characterizes the intuitive or Kantian moral theory is its claim that moral principles can be known by their form and are not dependent on experience or consequences for their validation. In contrast to this, Mill claims that inductive principles of morality are utterly derived from experience and are validated by the consequences. He argues that the inductive principles are superior because the intuitive principles fail for one of two reasons. Either the intuitive principles take up the everyday precepts of morality – Do not lie. Do not cheat. Do not steal, etc. – and assume that they are intuitive, or some abstract principle is proposed that supposedly grounds and accounts for all the everyday precepts. The problem with the first case is that the intuitive nature of the principles is assumed and not argued for, and Mill thinks it much more reasonable to suppose that these precepts were acquired through experience and weighing the consequences. The problem with the second case is that the principle is so abstract and unwieldy that people do not really follow that principle. They simply follow everyday precepts. Imagine being at home as a child on a long summer's day. You are getting ready to run outside to play. Just before the door closes, you hear your mom yell, "Don't act on any maxims that you couldn't at the same time will that they become universal!" Mill's point is that while this might give you pause, there's nothing you can act on here. When faced with a decision, you will resort to everyday maxims, such as "Be good." Mill thus concludes that inductive principles are superior to intuitive principles (11–12).

Everyone is a utilitarian (even Kant)

Mill has, so far, come to two conclusions: moral reasoning requires a principle, and thus far there has been no explicit agreement about either the nature or the content of such a principle, though his arguments lead him to prefer what he calls an "inductive" principle of morality. His preferences aside, these conclusions lead Mill to wonder whether any real harm has been caused by the absence of explicit agreement concerning a principle of morality. It is at this point that Mill notices something remarkable. There is, in fact, widespread agreement throughout history and across cultures concerning right and wrong. Most cultures throughout history have frowned upon lying, cheating, murder, and stealing. Most cultures throughout history have valued friendship, honesty, loyalty, and courage. We see broad acceptance of the Golden Rule (Do unto others as you would have them do unto you) in a dizzying array of societies, cultures, religions, and philosophy. Zoroastrianism has a version. Taoism has a version. The Upanishads, an ancient Hindu text, says, "Let no man do to another that which would be repugnant to himself; this is the sum of righteousness. A man obtains the proper rule by regarding another's case as like his own."[2] What accounts for this worldwide and historical agreement? Mill thinks this general agreement springs from an unacknowledged principle: namely, utilitarianism. That is, the reason there is such great overlap among moralities throughout history and across culture is that all of them unknowingly agree that the good = happiness = pleasure. Even Kant (12).

Perhaps the most surprising thing about Mill's claim here is not that he made it, but that Kant did not rise from his grave and take his revenge on Mill for making the claim in the first place. Mill begins his argument by claiming that everyone acknowledges the importance of pleasure or happiness in shaping people's actions. This seems indisputably true. Everyone wants to be happy. Everyone desires pleasure. This was already old news when Aristotle was writing. Even Kant admits this. Where everyone parts ways with Mill, though, is in drawing the conclusion that everyone *wanting* something makes it *right*. Undaunted, however, Mill explicitly takes up Kant's categorical imperative, as an example of extreme opposition, to show that secretly he is a utilitarian. As we saw, Kant argues that moral worth depends on the intentions behind the action not the consequences of an action, and we test our intentions by the categorical imperative. In the first

---

[2] Gensler et al., *Ethics: Contemporary Readings*, p. 159.

formulation of the categorical imperative a maxim passes or fails the test depending on whether the maxim can take the form of universal law. Admittedly, this formulation of the categorical imperative is often read as if Kant were saying, "If everyone did this, would the world be a better or worse place?" Mill does so here when he claims, "All he [Kant] shows is that the *consequences* of their [the maxims'] universal adoption would be such as no one would choose to incur" (13). This is difficult to square with Kant's insistence that consequences cannot be a guide to moral worth, since we have no control over the consequences.

Instead of resolving this conflict, though, I want to highlight the terms of the conflict, since Kant and Mill have very different ways of pursuing right action. One way we can think about this conflict is in terms of the distinction between the universal and the general. Kant clearly thinks that he is articulating the *universal* principle of morality, while Mill clearly thinks that he is articulating the *general* principle of morality. "Universal" has two related meanings for Kant. It is "formal" and "exceptionless." For Kant, as we saw, the only way we can be certain about being good is if we remove morality from the uncertainty of consequence and experience. What these means is that we examine our intentions or maxims to see if their form achieves what we called "lawlikeness" in the Kant section. This test is purely formal and it produces moral laws that are certain and exceptionless. The model here is something like the Pythagorean Theorem, $a^2+b^2=c^2$, which works for every right triangle without exception. As such, it is a *universal* law.

In contrast to Kant here, Mill does not think that moral laws can rise to this level of certainty. Past experience tells us what most of the people most of the time have done and whether actions of this type tend to produce more or less pleasure. This is a *general* law, but it also admits of exceptions. That is, past experience does not absolutely guarantee future consequences. Rather, past experience allows us to deal with consequences in terms of probability or likelihood. Thus, I can know with a high degree of probability that stealing will work out badly for all involved. What I cannot rule out, though, is the possibility that stealing might, on very rare occasions, produce more pleasure than pain: say, stealing medicine to save a sick child. A general principle can suggest degrees of probability, but because the moral worth of an action depends on the consequences, in the end we have to wait and see what happens in order to judge whether an action was good (82–3).

Utility and pleasure

We do not often use the words "utility" and "pleasure" interchangeably. In fact, they have come in many cases to have an opposed meaning. Perhaps this is a colloquialism but, when I was growing up, my family called the room with cleaning supplies and the washing machine, "the utility room." No one ever considered calling it "the pleasure room" because nothing about the room connotes pleasure. It was a workroom. From Mill's perspective, though, pleasure is precisely that which is most useful. Eating, drinking, and breathing are not only useful but pleasurable. We are driven towards pleasure and away from pain. Seeking pleasure keeps us alive and allows us to avoid injury. Utility is not opposed to this; it is equivalent to it. In this light, we can update Mill's formula to this:

$$Good = Happiness = Pleasure = Utility$$

All of these terms are equivalent for Mill. That is why he can call his moral principle "the principle of utility" or "the greatest happiness principle." Each is synonymous with the other (15–16).

As we noted above, though, all of these equivalences make it difficult for Mill to solve a basic problem in philosophy: namely, it seems obvious that people pursuing pleasure do the wrong thing sometimes. But if pleasure is the good, how can this be? Mill's answer to this objection is found in his formulation of the principle of utility, "the greatest happiness for the greatest number." Mill can thus grant that people sometimes pursue their own happiness at the expense of other people's happiness. However, the principle would rule out such an action as having moral worth. If pursuing my pleasure causes other people pain, then the principle of utility tells me that I have done the wrong thing. The principle of utility would also suggest that in future situations where I have a choice between my own pleasure and the pleasure of others, the pleasure of others should trump my own pleasure. Utility demands that I examine not just my own pleasure but also the total amount of pleasure generated by my actions. To the degree that my actions increase everyone's pleasure they are right, and to the degree that they decrease everyone's pleasure they are wrong (16).

Mill's first strategy in dealing with pleasure is to make a distinction between the pleasures we pursue for our own sake and the pleasures we pursue for the sake of others. His second strategy is to complicate his view of pleasure even further by distinguishing between two kinds of pleasure. The possibility of distinguishing between two kinds of pleasure arises from an ambiguity in the formulation of the principle of utility. In the phrase "the greatest happiness," "greatest" can mean two things. It can mean "the most" or "the best." Each meaning leads to a different account of the principle of utility. Those who argue for the most pleasure for the most people are known as "quantitative utilitarians." Those who argue for the best kind of pleasure for the most people are known as "qualitative utilitarians." Mill is a qualitative utilitarian, and thus believes not only that is there more than one kind of pleasure, but also that these kinds of pleasure can be ranked according to their superiority (18).

For Mill there are two basic kinds of pleasure, pleasures of the mind and pleasures of the body. Pleasures of the body would include things like eating, drinking, sex, and sports. Pleasures of the mind would include things like reading, conversation, art, science, and teaching. Mill thinks that the pleasures of the mind are superior to pleasures of the body. We could generate lots of reasons why this might be the case, but for Mill they all boil down to the fact that pleasures of the mind are more likely to produce better consequences. We can see this very clearly in the old adage, "Give a man a fish, and he will eat for a day. Teach a man to fish, and he will eat for a lifetime." Teaching is not only pleasurable in itself; it multiplies pleasure as those who learn not only do, but teach others, as well (18–19).

Mill's two strategies for dealing with the problem of pleasure can be summarized in the following table:

	Self	Others
Mind	Reading	Teaching others to read
Body	Eating	Cooking for others

We can note several important things about Mill's claims here. First, notice that the two ways of thinking about pleasure get combined here. The quantitative way of thinking about pleasure is expressed in the "Self" and "Others" columns. That is, it remains important for Mill to figure out where the pleasure is being directed. The direction of pleasure, however, is secondary in comparison to the type of pleasure, the "Mind" and "Body" rows, its qualitative dimension. It is this privileging of pleasure's quality over its quantity that makes Mill a qualitative utilitarian. What this means in practice is that personal pleasures of the mind are to be preferred over social pleasures of the body. That is, Mill thinks it is more likely that personal pleasures of the mind will ultimately produce more happiness than social pleasures of the body (19–20).

Why might this be the case? Part of the issue lies with the very nature of bodily pleasures. Let's say I cook a very special dinner for friends and family. While we are imagining, let's also imagine that it is very good. Everyone agrees it is the best meal they have ever had. Great, I have managed to produce a great deal of pleasure in quite a few people. According to the principle of utility, my actions have moral worth. What happens after the meal, though? Everyone goes home thoroughly satisfied. They go to bed, and they wake up hungry the next morning. Bodily pleasures, no matter how intense, do not last. They are ephemeral.

Compare the pleasure of a good meal to the pleasure of reading a book. We can grant that the pleasure of reading may not be as intense as a very good meal, but it is much more continuous and longer-lived. Reading a book may take a week or a month, while a meal lasts only an hour or two. Furthermore, reading may actually change me, make me see the world differently. Finally, and this is the most compelling part for Mill, reading can turn into conversation or teaching. That is, the personal pleasures of the mind can easily convert into the social pleasures of the mind in a way that the bodily pleasures cannot.

The important thing to remember in all of this is that Mill is not saying that the bodily pleasures are bad. He is not saying that bodily pleasures should be mitigated or avoided. What he is saying is that on those occasions when there is a conflict among the different kinds of pleasures, they can be ranked in this order – personal bodily, social bodily, personal mental, social mental – from least to most preferred.

That is, as the pleasures increase in rank they are more likely to produce greater happiness (22).

Objections

After defining the principle of utility, Mill spends the bulk of the second chapter addressing possible objections to utility as a guide for right action. Let's take a look at Mill's responses to some of the more salient objections. The first objection is that the utilitarian view of human nature makes us no better than animals. We can see this objection having its roots in Aristotle's view of human nature. As we saw, humans share being motivated by pleasure and pain with animals. If we are motivated solely by pleasure, we are no better than animals. Mill's response to this depends on his distinction between kinds of pleasures. There are pleasures that humans are capable of that animals are not. Utilitarianism says that pursuit of these higher, uniquely human pleasures is preferable to the pursuit of lower, animal pleasures. In fact, he goes so far as to say that pursuit of these higher pleasures is worthwhile, even if we fail to reach our goals. "It is better to be a human being dissatisfied than a pig satisfied; better to be Socrates dissatisfied than a fool satisfied" (20).

We do not always live up to our capacity for the higher pleasures of the mind, though. In fact, Mill is willing to admit that some people have lost the ability to take pleasure in the higher pleasures at all. The reason people might lose their capacity for the higher pleasures comes down to education, which echoes Aristotle's claim that proper education consists in being taught to feel pleasure and pain at the right things. Without proper education people can become insensitive to the higher pleasures and even disdain them. Friends and culture can reinforce this disdain for the higher pleasures until one's society becomes positively anti-intellectual. For Mill, the solution to this problem lies in a free and equal education for everyone (20–1).

Another objection to utilitarianism is that in the heat of the moment there is no time to weigh the possible consequences before acting. Mill's response is that we do not live in a vacuum. We live in a world with a long history that can be used as a guide to the likely consequences of our actions. Obviously, we can learn from our own experience, but we can learn from the experience of others without going through the pain of unexpected consequences. Art, literature, and religion can also be guides to likely consequences. Through great works of art and sacred texts we can test actions vicariously. Exposure to sources such as these is key to a good education. We can learn them as lessons before we act, so that our actions are likely to bring about the best consequences (35–7).

Some object that the principle of utility is too easily abused. It is far too easy, they claim, to generate arguments to show that what one wants to do is also what one ought to do. For example, let's say I am sitting in my office debating whether to go home early to relax or continue working on my class preparations for the next day. Obviously, going home is much more appealing, so I reason: Well, if I stay later and work harder, I will become more tired. The more tired I am, the more likely it is that I will get in a wreck on the way home. If I wreck on the way home, I will be injured, other people might be injured, my family will be distressed, and I will not be able to teach the next day. Since these consequences are so terrible, I am duty-bound to go home immediately and relax. The principle of utility proves it. Mill does not deny that this kind of perversion of the principle of utility is possible, but this possibility is not a problem with the principle of utility. It is a problem with human nature. Humans by nature are always looking for short cuts, and they are always looking for some way to rationalize those short cuts. All moralities have this problem, not just utilitarianism (37–8).

Now that Mill has given the principle of utility as the criterion for judging right action and responded to some common objections to it, he can proceed to other related matters. For example, even if there is some kind of tacit consensus surrounding the principle of utility, why should we obey it? Where does its authority come from? Also, even if the principle of utility can be shown to have some authority, why should it be the sole authority? In short, what proof can Mill give that the principle of utility is the highest arbiter of human action? Finally, what about justice? Is justice not so fundamentally distinct from happiness that it warrants its own set of principles? To paraphrase our discussion of Kant, is being good not just more important than being happy? We will see how Mill responds to these questions in the next chapter.

Summary

The rightness of an action depends on how much pleasure is produced. The greater the pleasure, the better the action. This is the principle that has guided human morality for millennia. Mill makes it explicit and calls it the principle of utility.

Questions

1. Are pleasure/goodness/happiness equivalent?
2. Are high pleasures to self superior to low pleasures to others?
3. What are the advantages and disadvantages of having a *general* principle of morality, as opposed to a *universal* principle of morality?

8

Mill: The Greatest Happiness for the Greatest Number
(*Utilitarianism*, Chapters 3, 4, and 5)

Key terms

Sanction – Authorization.

Happiness – The concrete aggregate of things one cannot live without.

Right – That which we are justified in demanding that others defend in us.

Justice – The pursuits most likely to secure happiness. Justice is not opposed to happiness but part of it.

Mill begins the third chapter of *Utilitarianism* speaking about the "ultimate sanction of the principle of utility." The word "sanction" seems odd in this context. The most common way that the word "sanction" is used today is in the phrase "economic sanctions." Economic sanctions, though, are economic penalties that states impose on other states, a refusal (relating to some products) to buy from or sell to the state on which sanctions are opposed. For example, the United States has long employed economic sanctions on Iran in order to gain some measure of political influence, as well as limit the development of nuclear technology. Within this context, Mill's search for the "sanction of utility" sounds strange. In fact, it sounds as if he is looking to limit or penalize utility in some way. This would be a surprising outcome (to say the least) for a book arguing that the principle of utility is the highest good.

Fortunately for Mill, there are other uses of the word "sanction." We are less familiar with these uses but may have come across them in a phrase such as "sanctioned by." In this case, "sanction" means to "approve of" or "authorize." In many religions, for example, marriage is sanctioned by the gods or God. That is, marriage is a public rite in which two people are joined. That joining is divinely authorized. We also speak about sporting events having this kind of sanction. For example, the location of the three-point line in basketball varies depending on which organization sanctions the game. A game sanctioned by the organization of colleges in the United States (the National Collegiate Athletic Association, or NCAA) will have a different three-point line from a game sanctioned by the professional basketball league in the US (the National Basketball Association, or NBA). Both of these three-point lines will differ from games sanctioned by the International Olympic Committee. In every case, though, the governing body authorizes or sanctions the rules of the game, and games played outside that sanction remain unofficial.

The sanction of utility

Mill's problem here is somewhat more complicated than where the three-point line goes. He wants to know what authorizes the principle for all right action. That is, given the fact that everyone wants to be happy, what compels us to pursue the greatest happiness for the greatest number? Or, to put the question more starkly, why do I sometimes sacrifice my pleasure for the sake of other people's pleasure? It turns out that, for Mill, there are two basic reasons for behavior like this: external and internal sanctions. There are two external sanctions for the principle of utility: hope of favor and fear of others' displeasure. Why do I sometimes sacrifice my pleasure for the sake of other people's pleasure? Because I hope to gain their favor if I do, and I fear their displeasure when I do not. Why do people do the right thing? Mill's claim is that one of the pressures on our behavior is that we worry what people will think of us. From the very earliest age we seek the praise of our family and then later our peers. This desire for praise requires us to seek the pleasure of others. By the same token, we also fear disappointing our family and peers. Growing up, the thing I feared most, much more than my parents' anger, was disappointing them, failing to live up to their expectations. One of the most devastating weapons in a parent's arsenal is to say, "I'm not mad, I'm just disappointed in you." That really cuts to the quick (40–1).

The internal sanction for utility springs from a sense of duty. For Mill, it is frankly irrelevant where this sense of duty comes from. We may locate it in religion, family, or state. One of the reasons why Mill thinks the source of duty is irrelevant is because, as we have seen, he thinks that at bottom all sources of duty arise from the principle of utility. In this instance, though, the irrelevance of the source follows from the fact that the internal sanction of utility is provided by the feelings that accompany the performance or violation of duty. As we will see below, duty provides us with a sense of obligation. We find it pleasurable to live up to our obligations and painful to violate our obligations. We are proud of ourselves when we do the right thing and ashamed of ourselves when we do the wrong thing (41–2).

What the external and internal sanctions for the principle of utility share is their common origin in the feelings of pleasure and pain. As Mill has maintained all along, pleasure and pain are the principal motivators of human activity. Where Mill differs from the other thinkers we have read is in his contention that actions are judged on the amount and quality of pleasure produced. In this chapter, he adds the additional claim that what authorizes the use of the principle of utility in judging the rightness of actions is the fact that pleasure (of self and others) arises from following it and pain (of self and others) arises from violating it. While some might argue that Mill's reasoning is circular here, Mill would maintain that his commitment to the fundamental psychology of pleasure and pain is thorough and consistent. Mill never seeks a ground outside of pleasure and pain on which to anchor his philosophy. He only seeks to show that our behavior, as well as our judgments about our behavior, all follow either directly or indirectly from pleasure and pain.

Mill is not quite out of the woods yet. It is very easy to see why people pursue their own pleasure. Their interest is obvious. It is also very easy to see why people might complain about other people selfishly pursuing their own pleasure. The complaints arise only when your pursuit of your pleasure interferes with my pursuit of my pleasure. All that is required for this dynamic is that people selfishly pursue their own desires. This is not Mill's claim, though. Mill's claim is that everyone has tacitly accepted the principle of utility – that people believe that goodness lies in the pursuit of the greatest happiness for the greatest number. The problem that Mill needs to solve, then, is selfishness. Why does Mill need the principle of utility, when selfishness seems to account for the same data much more elegantly?

Mill's answer to this question strikes right at the heart of easy assumptions that we make about ourselves and our relations to one another. It is easy to assume, for example, that the most important thing about us is our individuality. Everything about us, from shopping to ethics to politics, becomes an expression of that individuality. Western liberal democracies rising out of the social contract theories of Hobbes, Locke, and Rousseau enshrine the individual as the locus of rights that must be protected by the state. The individual is imagined as this fully-formed, discrete entity that comes on the scene without antecedent and without any essential connection to others. On this model, any connections an individual makes are voluntary.

Mill disputes this characterization of the individual and argues instead that humans are fundamentally social creatures. Humans are not separate atoms that only accidentally come into contact with others. No, humans are essentially related to other humans. We do not begin our lives in a vacuum. We begin our lives in a family. We need others, and others need us. As a result, Mill argues that, as humans, we have natural "social feelings." These social feelings form a counterbalance to our natural selfishness. We have a natural desire to seek our own pleasure, but we also have a natural desire "to be in unity with our fellow creatures" (45). This desire for unity checks our selfishness and urges us to seek a path that is beneficial to all.

Mill admits that people may be more or less sensitive to this social feeling. He is confident, though, that the path to sensitizing oneself to this social feeling is cultivation through proper education. One may begin life with a social feeling that extends only to one's immediate family. Through education, though, the sympathetic connection to others may be increased and continually widened until one sees that personal happiness is indeed bound up with the happiness of all (46).

Utility's proof

Mill mentions in the first chapter that the principle of utility cannot be proved in any usual sense of the term. He returns to that issue in the fourth chapter and admits that, in general, first principles cannot be arrived at by deduction. Here he sounds very much like Aristotle, arguing that some principles cannot be reached through argument but must be simply grasped. Mill, however, does not locate the principle of utility among the principles that must be grasped intuitively by a special mental faculty. His strategy is one of negative proof. That is, he states his position clearly and attempts to disprove it. When he discovers that it cannot be disproved, he concludes that his original position is true. As Mill freely admits, this kind of proof does not work like a proof in geometry or logic, but he thinks it is the best we can do with regard to a first principle, such as the principle of utility (49).

Here is Mill's claim: "The utilitarian doctrine is that happiness is desirable, and the only thing desirable as an end; all other things being only desirable as a means to that end" (49). Mill's claim here actually has two parts. The first part, "happiness is desirable," is straightforward and easily proved. We can prove this by simply asking ourselves, Do we want to be happy? If we were to list all the things we wanted, would happiness make the list? Since our discussion of Aristotle, it has been clear that everyone wants to be happy. This has never been in dispute. The real difficulty comes in the second part, where Mill claims that happiness is the *only* thing we want. The "only" here really raises the difficulty level on Mill's proof. As the formulation of a claim it has the great advantage of being proved false with one counterexample. That is, if we can think of one thing that we want that is not happiness or does not lead to happiness, then Mill's argument collapses. Everything we want is either happiness or the means to happiness (50).

In order to test his claim, particularly the stronger part of it, Mill examines two possible counterexamples, money and virtue. We will look at only virtue in depth. Is it not possible to love virtue or excellence for its own sake as an end, regardless of whether it is connected to happiness? While opposing virtue and happiness would have been unthinkable for Aristotle and Spinoza, in many ways Mill is reposing Kant's question, Is it better to be good or happy? In this case, though, "virtue" replaces "good." As we have seen, though, Mill's response is very different. Ultimately, his claim is that virtue is both desirable for its own sake and, as such, part of our overall happiness. Mill's argument here is complex, and it will ultimately force us to reevaluate the nature of happiness. In the first part of his argument, he admits that virtue can be desired for its own sake. This admission seems to be fatal to his claim. Here we clearly have something desired for its own sake that is not happiness, except that Mill saves his claim by disputing the idea that virtue is not happiness. How can he do this? While Mill clearly has moral virtue in mind, let's illustrate this using a more concrete example of excellence: musical skill. Let's imagine someone who loves music for its own sake, and who pursues musical excellence with passion and discipline. Based on this, let's imagine two scenarios. In the first scenario, our committed musician has worked very hard on a piece, but when it comes time to perform, it goes very badly. Is she happy? Obviously not. In the second scenario, let's imagine that a tragic accident prevents her from playing again. What effect does this have on her overall happiness? It diminishes it greatly, at least for a while. What might we conclude from these scenarios? We might conclude that the things that we pursue with passion and discipline are things that are not merely conducive to our happiness but part of it. That is, what we pursue most assiduously is not simply a means to our happiness; it is constitutive of our happiness (51–2).

Let's take a step back for a moment to compare Mill's position to the other thinkers that we have read. For Aristotle and Spinoza, there was an identity of goodness and happiness. For Kant, there was an opposition between goodness and happiness. Here, Mill puts goodness and happiness in a part/whole relation. This means that, on Mill's model, we can pursue an indefinite number of goods for their own sake. None of these would be opposed to happiness. They would all simply be parts of our happiness, that set of pursuits without which we could not be happy. This is the meaning behind Mill's claim, "Happiness is not an abstract idea, but a concrete whole" (53). In order to illustrate this further, let's think briefly about concrete, the stuff sidewalks are made of. It has probably been a long time since you examined the sidewalk closely, but if you will recall, it is not uniform but made up of little bits of varying size and shape. These little bits are fused together by a liquid medium (cement) that has hardened over time. For Mill, happiness is concrete in this precise sense. Our happiness is not a single undifferentiated thing but an aggregate of all the things that we could not be happy without. Happiness is composed and heterogeneous, not uniform and homogeneous. Furthermore, Mill grants that different people will compose their happinesses differently, even though the fundamental boundaries of pleasure and pain will remain.

With Mill's shift to happiness as a concrete whole, it becomes difficult to see how one might refute his claim that happiness is the only thing desirable as an end. If whatever we desire for its own sake is simply part of our overall happiness, then, by definition, happiness is the only thing we desire. Mill's claim about the relation between what ends we desire and happiness is analogous to the relation between white light and individual colors on a spectrum. There is no color on the spectrum that is not part of white light. White light is nothing but the composition of all the colors on the spectrum. It would be impossible to discover or create a color that did not already belong somewhere on the spectrum, and as a component of the spectrum it would be part of white light. A whole necessarily contains its parts. Whatever is desirable is desirable as a part of happiness. Therefore, happiness is the only thing desirable (53–4).

Utility and justice

The final chapter of *Utilitarianism* takes up what Mill takes to be the greatest obstacle to the explicit adoption of the principle of utility. This obstacle is the idea that right and wrong are not distinguished by happiness but by justice. Mill spends quite some time looking at current ideas around justice and their historical antecedents. As he lists some contemporary uses of the terms "just" and "unjust," numerous notions such as fairness and equality arise, but there does not seem to be anything holding them together. In the hopes of finding some unifying thread, Mill turns to the etymology of "justice." Here he discovers the notion of "right." With the notion of right come two related concepts, obligation and what we would call today "human rights." The connection between right and obligation is straightforward. Doing what is right or just appears to us as something we ought to do. The claims of justice have a compelling force behind them that give us pause before we act. For example, recently, the head of a drug company, Martin Shkreli, raised the price of a drug the company bought the rights to from $13.50 per pill to $750 per pill, an increase of over 5,000 percent. The outcry was immediate and loud. Initially, Shkreli claimed that he would not lower the price. Later, under intense pressure from every conceivable media outlet, he relented and agreed to lower the price. In this case, the public felt that Shkreli had violated his obligation to society, particularly the vulnerable in society, and did not hesitate to loudly denounce this violation (59–60).

The other connection between right and human rights is less straightforward. It may seem obvious, at first, but the idea of human rights is a fairly recent invention. The idea of human rights arises in the same period as the social contract theories of Hobbes, Locke, and Rousseau. All these theorists, along with Mill and Kant, claim that rights are not just a property of actions but a property of individuals. That is, I possess my rights simply by being human. For Locke, for example, these rights would include, life, liberty, and property. Different thinkers argue about the exact nature and content of these rights but all agree that these rights are connected to our freedom. Freedom lies in the protection of these rights, and unfreedom lies in the violation of these rights. Thus, rights are that which reside in each of us and which all others are obligated to protect. Within this context, most theories of government seek the best way to protect these rights. The point of the American Declaration of Independence makes this explicit. It states, "We hold these truths to be self-evident, that all men are created equal, that they are endowed by their Creator with certain unalienable Rights, that among these are Life, Liberty and the pursuit of Happiness." The argument presented in the document is that Great Britain had failed in its duties to uphold these rights, and this is sufficient justification for revolution. The connection that Mill needs in order to tie up all these senses of justice and right is obligation. Even though talking about this obligation in terms of human rights is new, the idea that we owe something to one another is very ancient indeed (67).

For Mill, the obligation that we have to one another can be traced back to the "social feeling" that we discussed earlier. The basic question remains, though. Are the feelings of obligation that have been codified in the discourse of human rights not different in kind from happiness? Is Mill not forced to admit two basic principles of action: justice and utility? He thinks not. While Mill can fall back on some of his previous arguments in order to answer this charge, his immediate response is that the only possible reason why we ought to defend the rights of others is utility. A society that fails to protect all its members equally not only is an unjust society, but also it is an unhappy society. An unhappy society is much more likely to revolt than a happy one (71).

On Mill's reading, justice is not opposed to happiness. To echo the previous chapter, it is part of our happiness. The supposed opposition between justice and happiness arises because the dictates of justice are so extraordinarily important to the general welfare. As Mill writes, "It appears from what has been said that justice is a name for certain moral requirements which, regarded collectively, stand higher in the scale of social utility, and are therefore of more paramount obligation, than any others" (82). The tendency we have to shout "Hey, no fair!" that begins in our earliest childhood continues throughout our whole lives. When we are not being treated fairly we are quick to remind others of their obligations. Why? Everyone's happiness depends on it (77).

Exceptions

In the previous chapter we characterized the difference between Kant's and Mill's moral theories in terms of the difference between the universal and the general. Mill drives this point home in the conclusion to *Utilitarianism* when he writes, "though particular cases may occur in which some other social duty is so important, as to overrule any one of the general maxims of justice" (82). We will look at Mill's specific examples in a moment, but for now let's look at his claim here. To begin with, he supposes "general maxims of justice." Notice that he calls them "general" not "universal." As we saw, "general" means "for most of the people most of the time." So, in this case, "general maxims of justice" must mean "those rules that usually best satisfy our obligations to one another." We can imagine all sorts of rules that fit the bill here: Do not steal. Do not kill. Do not force people to do things they do not want to do. Following these rules usually promotes the general happiness. However, Mill is willing to admit that there may be occasions when other social duties overrule the general maxims of justice. What does Mill have in mind here? "Thus, to save a life, it may not only be allowable but a duty to steal or take by force the necessary food or medicine, or to kidnap and compel to officiate the only qualified medical practitioner" (82). Just to be absolutely clear here, Mill is saying that, in extreme, life-or-death circumstances, we may have a *duty* to steal, rob, or kidnap. We may be *obligated* to do these things. We would be wrong *not* to do them.

Notice that Mill's claim is not that desperate people sometimes do desperate things. His claim is that, in a given situation, doing the desperate thing is the *right* thing to do. This is a far cry from Kant's moral theory, which could certainly allow that desperate people might do desperate things, but they would never be right or obligated to do such things. Kant's universal theory of morality can admit of no exceptions, whereas Mill's general theory of morality can admit of exceptions. The obvious problem with Kant's theory is that it seems too rigid. We tend to think of rules as always having exceptions. The obvious problem with Mill's theory is that he offers almost no guidelines with regard to when an exception to the general rules of justice might be employed. It seems clear from his example that saving a life trumps many typical rules of justice. How far should we go, though? Would it be acceptable to forcibly take a kidney from one person in order to save the life of someone dying with kidney failure? Would it be acceptable to kill one person and harvest his organs in order to save seven people?

Mill's response here would no doubt be twofold. In the case of the more extreme examples, especially killing one person to save seven, Mill would claim that a society that allowed such a violation of one person would not be a society that promotes the general happiness. People would live in fear that they would be next. At the same time, and precisely because his principles are general rather than universal, he could not rule out the possibility absolutely. Here he runs up against Kant's criticism that the consequences of an action are unpredictable and uncontrollable. We can never say with certainty what will produce the greatest happiness because the consequences are too difficult to predict. Mill accepts these limitations and thinks that we will continue to learn from experience and, as a result, continually improve in our abilities to act in a way that produces the greatest happiness for the greatest number (82–3).

Mill's moral theory thus begins with what everyone admits: namely, that everyone wants to be happy. Where Mill diverges from the other thinkers we have read is in equating happiness with pleasure and arguing that the pursuit of pleasure is, in fact, the highest good. He adds two important qualifications to the pursuit of pleasure, though. First, for Mill, there are different kinds of pleasure, pleasures of the body and pleasures of the mind, and it is better to pursue pleasures of the mind. Second, we may pursue pleasures directed solely at the self or directed at others. When these two directions conflict, it is better to pursue the pleasure of others. Mill's contention is that the principle that seeks the greatest happiness for the greatest number already lies at the root of all our actions. His only task is to make this implicit assumption explicit, so that we can reason in a principled way about right action.

Summary

Happiness is the only thing people desire, because happiness is a concrete whole composed of everything we pursue for its own sake. Justice is not opposed to happiness but the most important part of this concrete whole.

Questions

1. Is happiness a concrete whole?
2. Is it better to pursue justice than happiness?
3. When is it our duty to kidnap a doctor?

PART III BEYOND

HOW MIGHT WE LIVE?
NIETZSCHE AND LEVINAS

Beyond

The two philosophers that we will read about in this section are Nietzsche and Levinas. Friedrich Nietzsche (1844–1900) is probably best known for saying "God is dead." His writings were also later used by the Nazis to support their claims of superiority. As we will see, though, superiority for Nietzsche can never arise out of hatred and resentment. Hatred and resentment are signs of weakness, never signs of strength. For Nietzsche, greatness can arise only in the affirmation of life. This is the lens through which he examines the entire history of morality. Does morality affirm or deny life? For the most part, Nietzsche thinks that morality denies life.

Emmanuel Levinas (1906–95) is not nearly as well known as Nietzsche. However, his philosophy provides an interesting and powerful contrast. Levinas, a Jewish émigré from Lithuania, was one of the first people to introduce the new German philosophy called "phenomenology" to France. Then World War II broke out. Levinas fought in the French army until he was captured by German soldiers and sent to a prisoner-of-war camp. There, in the midst of war, he began working on his philosophy, which begins with a critique of all of Western philosophy and ends with an ethical relation in which the needs of the other person take complete priority over my needs.

What both Nietzsche and Levinas have in common is their starting point. Both begin with a critique of Western thought, but each draws a different conclusion from his critique. Nietzsche concludes that Western thought has been life-denying, while Levinas concludes that Western thought has been unethical. In the face of their sweeping critiques, we can see both philosophers attempting to respond to a new question. Neither "How should we live?" nor "How should we act?" is sufficient. Both of those questions leave too many assumptions unexamined. Nietzsche and Levinas think that the key to philosophy lies in going beyond past forms of thought in order to generate something new. Thus, their question is "How might we live?"

This question adds another dimension to our philosophy. It requires that we look for trends or commonalities across large swaths of history. It is only when we understand these larger trends that we can imagine how things might be done differently. The first two sections of this book, then, become the necessary preparation for the third section. It is only by understanding "what is" that we can go "beyond."

9

Nietzsche: These are the Wrong Questions
(*Genealogy of Morals*, First Essay)

Key terms

Philology – The historical study of languages.
Genealogy – Nietzsche's method. It seeks the origin and value of philosophical terms.
Resentment – The hatred of the strong by the weak. Nietzsche uses the French "*ressentiment*."
Morality – Our current value system. It is organized around the opposition between "good" and "evil."

So far, we have seen that ethics is organized around the question How should we live? Aristotle and Spinoza articulated two different visions of philosophy, both oriented around this question. Morality, in contrast, is organized around the question How should we act? Kant and Mill both devised principles that would guide us to right action. Obviously, these questions are not mutually exclusive. Any philosophy worth the name will be able to answer both. The difference is one of emphasis and priority. For Aristotle and Spinoza, right action arises from living well, while, for Kant and Mill, living well arises from right action.

Nietzsche stands in stark contrast to these two basic ways of thinking about philosophy. For Nietzsche, these are the wrong questions and serve only to reproduce the same misconceptions about philosophy that have plagued it since its origins. In order to avoid these pitfalls, we need to think about philosophy differently. We need to ask whether or not the things valued by philosophy are *actually* valuable. To give a brief example, all of the philosophers that we have read up to this point have placed an unwavering and unquestioned faith in reason as the ground of philosophy. From Aristotle to Mill, no one seriously questions the importance of reason for living well or right action. The only question for these philosophers lies in the nature of reason and its proper use. Its value is never questioned. Nietzsche questions the value of reason, though. He questions everything we hold dear. Nietzsche does not want to redecorate the same 2,500-year-old house. He wants to tear the house down and start over again. Nietzsche's willingness to call everything into question makes him challenging to read, but it is also this willingness that makes him worth reading.

If we were to articulate a question around which Nietzsche's philosophy is oriented, it would not be "How should we live?" or "How should we act?" It would be "How *might* we live?" The "might" in this question signifies Nietzsche's desire to make something new with his life, to be creative. Nietzsche sees life as an art project and himself and the world as his canvas. What might he be capable of if he started with a blank canvas instead of one covered with two millennia of clichés about how one should live? What might we be capable of if we saw our past not as something to be lived up to, but as something to be overcome?

Nietzsche's method: genealogy

In order to avoid reproducing philosophy's past, Nietzsche proposes a new method for doing philosophy. This method is actually drawn from his training in the history of languages, called "philology." Philology is interested in the way in which languages are related to other languages. For example, in the late eighteenth century, work in the ancient Indian language of Sanskrit revealed numerous commonalities between Sanskrit and most European languages, including Greek and Latin. The obvious conclusion to be drawn from this is that Sanskrit and most European languages derive from a common source language, now known as "Indo-European." Philology draws two conclusions from this. First, languages evolve and develop over time. This conclusion gives impetus to a research program in philology that pursues mechanisms of change. Why, for example, does Latin become French in some places and Spanish in others? Philology seeks to answer questions like that. The second conclusion that philology draws from its study of the history of languages is that any given language points back to the ancestor languages from which it developed. Thus, while German is clearly part of the Indo-European language family, Hungarian is not. That is, even though Hungary is surrounded by Indo-European languages, its language is part of a different family tree.

Nietzsche takes the insights afforded by philology and applies them to philosophy. He seeks to do a "genealogy" of our moral terms. Where have our moral terms, such as "good" and "evil," come from? How have they developed over time? Given their source and development, what conclusions might we draw about their value? Both of the essays that we will look at in Nietzsche's *Genealogy of Morals* take up basic moral terms such as "good," "bad," and "guilt," and question their value. As Nietzsche points out, though, even the question of value is fraught. Not only must the question of value for what be asked, but also the question of value for whom. As far as Nietzsche is concerned there are no easy or obvious answers. The fact that everyone agrees about the value of something makes it more suspect, not less (Preface §3).[1]

Nietzsche's method also creates a terminological problem. The previous philosophers that we looked at all agreed that there was a highest good, and that this highest good was, in fact, "good." If Nietzsche is calling the value of "good" into question, though, how do we talk about that without losing ourselves in hopeless confusion? Is the "old good" "bad" and the "new good" "good"? In order to avoid this kind of confusion, Nietzsche generally replaces moral terms with physiological terms, such as "sickness" and "health." Thus, his question is not Is the "good" really "good"? His question is Have those things we have traditionally called "good" been healthy or harmful for us? Of course, this does not completely get Nietzsche out of the woods. "Healthy" and "harmful" still require further elucidation. What it does do, however, is avoid immediate confusion and shift the conversation from the moral register to the biological register. Ultimately, Nietzsche is much more

---

[1] There is no standardized reference system for Nietzsche's works. However, the *Genealogy of Morals* is helpfully divided into three essays, with each essay being further divided into sections. I will refer to the essay number followed its section number, or in the case of some references I refer to Nietzsche's Preface to the *Genealogy*.

interested in the ways that we are animals, than in the ways that we are separate from animals (Preface §3).

A genealogy of "good"

Nietzsche begins the first essay of the *Genealogy* baffled by the way in which an understanding of the "good" has been pursued. Here he singles out the "English psychologists" as particularly egregious in their shoddy "history of the good." For our purposes here, Mill will stand in nicely for the "English psychologists." The main problem with Mill's history of the good is that it is profoundly unhistorical. As we saw, Mill argues that "good" is the same through history and across culture. Nietzsche rejects Mill's just-so story as anachronistic projection. That is, Mill has taken the way we use the word "good" today and projected backwards onto all of history. What is the meaning of "good" that Mill projects? For Nietzsche, Mill's philosophy and morality in general boils down to the value of "unselfishness" and its closely allied concept, "equality." What was the principle of all morality, everywhere for Mill? The greatest happiness for the greatest number. That is, actions are right to the degree that they produce pleasure for others. Acting selfishly, without regard for the happiness of others, is the worst thing one can do. Furthermore, treating others unfairly or unequally strikes at the heart of justice, which, as we saw, Mill argues is the most important part of happiness (I, §§1–2).

From Nietzsche's perspective, Mill's claims should be easy to confirm or deny. We can actually look and see if the word "good" has always been used the way the Mill supposes. We have access to a wide range of ancient texts in Sanskrit, Greek, and Latin. How do these texts use the word "good"? Do they use the word "good" to refer to unselfish acts, acts that promote equality? No, they do not. What we discover instead is a world where "good" refers not to unselfish acts, but to people of high social rank. In the ancient world, "good acts" were simply those acts performed by "good people." Being a good person was determined by birth. The good were the "noble," "the high-born." They were the "warriors" and sometimes "priests." What Nietzsche thus discovers through his research is not a continuous valuation of unselfish acts, but two distinct moralities: an older morality that valued people of high social status and a newer morality that does, in fact, value unselfish acts. For Nietzsche, this generates two questions that his genealogical method is designed to answer. First, what caused the change from the old to the new morality? Second, has this development been healthy or unhealthy for us (I, §§4–5)?

In order to understand the causes that led to the shift in moralities, we need to flesh out both moralities a little further. If, in the old morality, the good were the high-born, who were the "bad"? Obviously, everyone of insufficiently noble birth is "bad." The world of the old morality is highly stratified. One's position in society is set at birth. One is born either "good" or "bad." One is born either "high" or "low." Thus, the other side of the ledger in the old morality includes "the low-born," "the plebeian," "the poor," "the rabble," "the masses" (I, §10).

In the new morality, goodness is not determined by social status. Goodness is determined by whether one acts sufficiently unselfishly. This morality is profoundly democratic. Anyone can be good. All that is required is acting in everyone's interest. What about selfish actions? What do we call those? Here Nietzsche notes a subtle shift in vocabulary. Acts that damage the common good and create inequality are not merely "bad," but "evil." Let's imagine someone who only acts selfishly and is completely bereft of what Mill called "social feeling." This is someone who only seeks his own gain and furthermore does not feel the least bit of guilt when he harms others in the pursuit of his own desires. Such behavior is "monstrous" or "inhuman." It is the defining characteristic of serial killers. We would say such a person is "evil" and a "psychopath." It would seem that the new morality, our current morality, is really intent on weeding out anti-social behavior and ensuring that everyone is treated as fairly as possible. Now that we have fleshed out both moralities, we can more easily compare and contrast them in two tables:

Old morality	
Good	**Bad**
Noble	Common
High-born	Low-born
Warrior	Peasant
Priest	Rabble

New morality	
Good	**Evil**
Unselfish acts	Selfish acts
Equality	Inequality
Common good	Good of the few
Democratic	Aristocratic

As we have discussed, the very meaning of the word "good" shifts from the old to the new morality. Furthermore, this shift in meaning is accompanied by a conceptual shift. The conceptual opposition between the good/bad of the old morality is very different from the good/evil opposition of the new morality. There are numerous ways that the prince is opposed to the pauper, but these are very different from the ways that Mother Theresa is opposed to the psychopath. These are qualitatively different oppositions. The old and new moralities are not simply mild variations of one another. They offer starkly different visions of the world. They value profoundly different things. They are so different that it is difficult to imagine how the new morality arises out of the old morality, but this is the problem Nietzsche must solve (Preface §6).

Out with the old

Nietzsche's proposed solution to the shift from the old to the new morality is resentment. The resentment of the "bad" lower class toward the "good" upper class generates what Nietzsche calls "the slave revolt in morality." Thus, from Nietzsche's perspective, the shift from the old to the new morality is a shift of power. In the old morality, the high caste held all the power. After the slave revolt, the plebeians take over and call themselves "good," relegating their former masters to the "evil" category. The mechanism for this revolution in power lies in the powerful psychological impetus of resentment (I, §10).

Resentment is a hatred that arises out of envy or inequality. We may hate for many different reasons, but we resent only those who have it better than us in some way. To the degree that we resent, we resent those with more money or fame or power. At bottom, resentment supposes that those we resent are somehow undeserving of their money, fame, or power. Take music, for example. There is a real tension in music appreciation between popularity and authenticity. Many argue that the more popular something is, the less likely it is to be authentic. And, of course, if it is inauthentic, then it cannot be good music. They will claim, "Taylor Swift is just manufactured pop music. There's no depth there. It's not REAL, man. Meanwhile, a great band like Deerhoof is tragically ignored."

Resentment becomes even clearer if we look at sports. It often happens that I am teaching Nietzsche about the time of the men's college basketball tournament, in which sixty-four teams compete for the national championship. I ask my students which team they hate the most, or which team they would most like to see go down in ignominious defeat in the first round. While there is some variability in the answer, the most common answer by far is Duke. Duke University is a college basketball powerhouse. They are always perennial favorites to do very well in the tournament. So, I ask the students, "Why do you hate Duke?" They answer without hesitation, "Because they always win." I ask them if they realize that they hate Duke *because* they are good. Instead of celebrating excellence, they despise it.

Our resentment always flows upward, never downward. The students that do not hate Duke hate some other excellent team, North Carolina or Kentucky. They never hate teams that only occasionally do well in the tournament, such as Davidson or George Mason. The same goes for other sports. In American football, people hate the dominant New England Patriots. Nobody hates the Arizona Cardinals. In World Cup soccer, people hate powerhouses such as Germany and Brazil but never hate struggling teams such as Cameroon or Japan. Resentment is a hatred of what appears to be superior. This hatred is especially strong when the reason for this apparent superiority is unclear or lacking.

Under the old morality, it became less and less clear to the commoners why they were participating in it. Who your parents were did not make you a good person. Neither your social circle nor money made you a good person. None of this changed the fact, however, that the nobles held all the power. What the commoners needed was somebody on the inside. At this point, the priestly class comes to the rescue, and they come to the rescue precisely because of the resentments they are harboring. What the priests really resent is the glory and honor bestowed on the warriors. The warriors get to go out and have all sorts of adventures. They bring home treasure from foreign lands and are lauded for their strength and bravery. Meanwhile, the priests have to stay home to perform rituals to appease the gods. This appeasement is only possible, of course, to the degree that the priests abstain from adventures that involve killing, raping, and pillaging. The priests think they are not getting enough credit for the work they are doing, and they resent the warriors for stealing credit for their victories. The warriors merely have to fight the battle. The priests do the hard work of ensuring victory by keeping the gods on their side (I, §6).

In order to exact their revenge on the warriors, though, the priests need to be clever. They cannot defeat the warriors in battle. Their victory must be subtle and spiritual. What do you do when you cannot win the game? Change the rules. Change the rules so that a new value takes hold. This new value defines "good" as "pure" and "bad" as "impure." Who determines who is pure? The priests. Who is most likely to be impure? The warriors. What must the warriors do in order to become pure? Submit to the priests. In this way, the priests gain the upper hand. They do not engage the warriors with strength; they change the value of strength by declaring the higher value of purity (I, §7).

The shift in value from strength to purity accomplished the intended task of giving the priests more power under the old morality. At the same time, this shift had the unintended consequence of weakening the boundary between social strata. Prior to this shift, goodness was inherited along with high social status. Once "purity" becomes the meaning of "good," however, it can be conferred on anyone of any social status. Anyone can be pure. Even the lowest-born person can undergo the rituals of purification. Goodness now shifts from a natural property to an acquired one. Goodness is no longer the sole province of nobility, but something that can be gained through right action. The boundaries between good and bad are now porous. Low birth is no longer an obstacle to reaching the highest levels of power.

What initially begins as a trickle becomes a flood as the path to advancement opens up to members of every class. Once the floodgate opens, the real revolution in morality occurs as the good/bad morality is replaced with the good/evil morality. The obvious question that arises is Why would a shift occur at all? Now that anyone can achieve power, why would morality not just stabilize around the pure/impure valuation? To answer these questions, Nietzsche returns to the power of resentment. Resentment does not simply want to equalize things. Resentment wants those we resent humiliated. It is not sufficient for Manchester United to lose occasionally. We want them to lose so badly for so long that they are kicked out of the Premier League. This attitude is borne out in repeated psychological experiments as well. When people are given a choice between lowering the salaries of their bosses to their level or raising their own salaries to the same level as their boss, they overwhelmingly choose to lower their bosses' salaries. Resentment has a real punitive edge to it (I, §9).

If resentment not only wants to level the playing field but also see the former victors punished, it will seek to change the rules so that those who were in power can never rise to power again. This is precisely what the new morality accomplishes. In the old morality, goodness flowed from the person. Good acts were simply acts done by good people. Good people were those born good. In the new morality, people are only good to the degree that their acts are good. The goodness of an act does not depend on who performs it. It depends on its unselfishness. That is, good acts are not those that affirm who I am, but those that negate who I am. I am good by virtue of not acting in my interest, by not calling attention to myself. Furthermore, my goodness depends on the assumption that everyone is equal. Everyone must be treated the same and to suggest that some people are better than others is downright evil. To say, "Do you know who I am?" is no longer a valid defense of one's actions. It does not matter who you are. Everyone is equal and goodness lies in unselfish actions (I, §13).

The morality of resentment

For Nietzsche, the impetus behind the shift from the old morality to the new is resentment. Furthermore, resentment reorganizes our values so that we place the highest value on things such as unselfishness, equality, humility, chastity, and poverty. The opposed values of selfishness, inequality, pride, promiscuousness, and wealth are not merely unfortunate side effects but to be actively shunned. The question that remains for Nietzsche's genealogical analysis is, Has the shift from the old to the new morality been healthy or unhealthy? For Nietzsche, resentment is profoundly unhealthy and so is the morality based on it (I, §16).

The reason that resentment is unhealthy is that it is what Nietzsche calls "life-denying." Resentment says "No" to life. Life is an experiment for Nietzsche, a creative endeavor. Living is a constant test of one's limits. We can place one of Nietzsche's best-known quotations from *Twilight of the Idols*, "What does not kill me makes me stronger," in this context ("Maxims and Arrows," 8). Living entails facing up to one's weaknesses and seeking to overcome them. We may not always succeed in overcoming our weaknesses, but in the attempt we shape ourselves (I, §10).

Resentment is life-denying because it drains life of its creativity. Resentment protects us from life rather than allowing us to live it. In order to illustrate this point Nietzsche recounts a fable of lambs and birds of prey.

> That lambs dislike great birds of prey does not seem strange: only it gives no ground for reproaching these birds of prey for bearing off little lambs. And if the lambs say among themselves: "these birds of prey are evil; and whoever is least like a bird of prey, but rather its opposite, a lamb – would he not be good?" there is no reason to find fault with this institution of an ideal, except perhaps that the birds of prey might view it a little ironically and say: "we don't dislike them at all, these good little lambs; we even love them: nothing is more tasty than a tender lamb." (I, §13)

There are several things to note about this parable. First, it is clear that the birds of prey are the nobles of the old morality and the lambs are the commoners. Second, Nietzsche's contention is that the new morality is one in which the lambs determine value. Third, the difference in value determination is striking. Notice that the birds of prey do not hate the lambs. In fact, they do not really think about them much at all. In contrast to this, the lambs' world is organized around their hatred of the birds of prey. The determination of "evil" comes first, and only on the basis of that determination do the lambs consider themselves good.

The fact that the lambs' self-understanding comes as a reaction to the determination of evil is the most telling part of Nietzsche's parable. This is why resentment is life-denying. If my first concern is with how hostile and dangerous the world is, I will live a life of fear and caution. I will not be creative because I am too scared to venture out into the world. My whole life will be consumed with hatred for the enemy that I need in order to define myself. Additionally, I will do everything in my power to ensure that my enemies cannot harm me. The chief rule of the new morality is that everyone must act like a commoner. The chief rule of the lambs' morality is that everyone must act like a lamb. Acting like a bird of prey is the greatest evil. My hatred takes the form of positing new values in which everyone must act like me or be evil. We cannot create or test ourselves in an environment like this. We do not even know who we are apart from our hatred. A morality predicated on resentment does not further life; it crushes life. Such a morality can only produce a hatred of life itself. This hatred of life, hatred of our own capabilities, is what Nietzsche calls "nihilism" (I, §12).

Thus, Nietzsche's genealogical method suggests that our current use of the word "good" cannot be simply projected through history and across cultures. "Good" used to mean something very different from what it means now. The shift between these two senses of the word "good" was caused by resentment. Our current values, the ones by which we organize the world, are founded on our feelings of inferiority. These values are designed to ensure that everyone feels equally inferior and never does anything about it. Nietzsche thinks we are harming ourselves by living this way. These values cause us to shrink away from testing ourselves and creating something new. The new morality is profoundly unhealthy (I, §14).

Given his criticisms of the new morality, it might be tempting to suppose that Nietzsche is arguing for a return to the old morality. While he certainly thinks that the new morality is unhealthy in comparison to the old morality, he does not think we can simply return to the old morality. We have lived under the new morality for too long. We have changed ourselves too much. We cannot repeat the past. Nietzsche's philosophy does not look backward to a lost golden age. It is a philosophy of the future. Nietzsche's hope for the future is that we will be able to overcome our current values and our current hatred of life. How might we live "beyond good and evil"? This is a question that Nietzsche takes up in the next essay, as well as in many of his other works.

Summary

Where did our current morality come from? Has it helped or hindered us? Nietzsche argues that our current morality arises out of resentment and has thus been harmful to us.

Questions

1. Nietzsche's genealogical method allows him to ask new questions about philosophy. Are these the right questions?
2. Is our current morality based on resentment?
3. What would it mean to "overcome" morality?

10

Nietzsche: Morality and Power
(*Genealogy of Morals*, Second Essay)

Key terms

Power – The ability or capacity of anything to establish and expand its area of control.

Debt – An economic relation whereby something is owed.

Guilt – A psychological/theological relation whereby non-economic debt is incurred.

Bad conscience – Turning our dominating instincts inward instead of outward.

In comparison to the other philosophers that we have read, Nietzsche is frustrating. He is frustrating because he seems much more interested in diagnosing the problem than he is in solving it. Some readers find this perspective unrelentingly negative. In contrast to Nietzsche, the other philosophers spend most of their time giving a clear account of how we are supposed to live or act. There are two reasons for Nietzsche's difference in perspective. First, his project differs in scope. Nietzsche is not simply trying to add his voice to the already crowded chorus of philosophy. He is not adding a subtle harmony to an already settled composition. Nietzsche is calling into question the very rules of composition. He wants to know why we compose the way that we do. The answer that he gives to the question of composition is "power." Everything, a canyon, an animal species, a building, language, a morality, is the expression of power. Or, better, everything is the expression of multiple competing powers. The old morality was the expression of the power of the few in accordance with social status. This power was able to keep in check the power of the many for a very long time. The new morality expresses a revolution in power that values its equal distribution. This distribution of power ideally prevents its concentration in the hands of the few. Thus, Nietzsche is not seeking to answer the question How can we make morality better? but Where did our morality come from?

The second reason for Nietzsche's difference in perspective follows from the first. Since his entire project begins by calling into question the very limits of morality, he is forced to talk about what lies beyond those limits. The problem with speaking about what lies beyond the limits of morality is that the values that constitute morality also constitute our ways of thinking and speaking. This means that Nietzsche can speak about what lies beyond the new morality only with the language of the new morality. As a result, Nietzsche will often speak elliptically and paradoxically about what lies beyond. Furthermore, he will often only be able to say what lies beyond is not. Whatever lies beyond our current system of values, by definition, must differ from it. Otherwise, it is not "beyond" in any relevant sense. This is why Nietzsche spends so much time in critique and so little time telling us how we should act.

Wolves and Chihuahuas

Nietzsche opens the Second Essay of the *Genealogy* with a provocative claim: Morality is a breeding program. The claim is provocative precisely because it connects two things we normally keep separate, our animal and spiritual natures. Normally, we think of morality as something that separates us from the animals. Here, Nietzsche is arguing that morality is shaping our animal natures. Importantly, though, morality is not shaping our animal natures by the way that reason controls individual impulses. Rather, morality is playing the role of a rancher selecting desirable traits in cattle. A rancher may select cattle for superior milk production or superior beef production. The process is long and arduous and requires the rancher to keep careful records of which cows have been bred (II, §1).

Nietzsche's claim begins to make more sense, though, if we think about the ways that morality drives mate selection in humans. One of the most important factors driving mate selection in humans is shared values. People are much more likely to make long-term commitments to those they feel share their values. Or, to put the matter in the starkest terms possible, no one wants to date (let alone marry) someone who is "evil." People only want to commit to people who are "good." The result is that "good" people produce offspring with other "good" people. These children are then raised "good" and, in turn, look for "good" mates. The slave revolt in morality has been continually reinforced genetically as "evil" has been systematically bred out of us. Thus morality is a breeding program, a selection of some kinds of power and the diminution of other kinds of power.

Nietzsche argued in the First Essay that the slave revolt in morality has been an unhealthy development for humans. Within the context of the Second Essay, we can illustrate Nietzsche's concerns clearly. Genetically, all dogs are descended from wolves. While it is not entirely clear how or when this happened, at some point humans began domesticating wolves, turning them into dogs. Thus, *Canis lupus* became *Canis lupus familiaris*. What is remarkable in this long history of domestication is the immense variety produced by the process of domestication. Ancient breeders selected traits to produce hunting and herding dogs. It produced hunting dogs that hunted by sight and tracking dogs that hunted by smell. It produced herding dogs that looked like sheep to better protect the sheep against wolves. It produced guard dogs and fighting dogs. Domestication even produced tiny companion dogs such as the Chihuahua. Breeding programs can thus introduce great changes in a species. Furthermore, a breeding program can become so successful that the products of the program can vastly outnumber the original lineage. This is clearly what has happened in the relation between wolves and dogs. Wolves used to vastly outnumber dogs. Now the opposite is true. What Nietzsche wants to know is what kind of development this has been for the wolf? Everyone can see that it is possible through selective breeding to turn a wolf into a Chihuahua. Has this been a healthy development for the wolf?

It is difficult to see any measure by which the Chihuahua is a healthier wolf than a wolf. Chihuahuas are frail and tiny. They shiver when they are nervous or cold. Owners are advised not to let them jump from the couch, since they might injure themselves. They are dependent on their owners for food and protection. It is not a breed that could survive long on its own in the wild. Of course, there are measures according to which humans might value Chihuahuas more. This is Nietzsche's entire point. A Chihuahua only becomes laudable under a different value system. This revolution in values requires that power be deployed differently. We created a world that values Chihuahua-like traits more than wolf-like traits. We instituted a breeding program that emphasized some traits and de-emphasized others. Humans are the result of a similar breeding program (II, §1).

The right to make promises

The particular trait that most interests Nietzsche is the "right to make promises." The right to make promises is contrasted in the opening sections of the Second Essay with the ability to make promises. For Nietzsche, the moral breeding program that we have foisted on ourselves has created only the ability to make promises, not the right to make promises. Our morality has created the ability to make promises by making us "calculable, regular, necessary" (*Genealogy* II, 1). In short, our morality has made us predictable, and it is this predictability that gives us the ability to make promises. I can make promises about my own behavior, in large part, because I know what kinds of actions I will take, and the way others will respond to those actions. I possess this knowledge about my actions and the actions of others because I assume they will, for the most part, act unselfishly and democratically. I can promise to give you a chocolate tomorrow, because I know that no one will steal them from the refrigerator in the lounge, even though they are not marked in any way. My promising depends on everyone's behavior being made predictable by morality.

Nietzsche's contention, though, is that such promises are not worth much. At least, they do not say anything praiseworthy about the person making the promise. In this situation, promises simply reflect the dominance of our current value system. Praising the making and keeping of promises in this environment is like praising Chihuahuas for being small. They have been bred that way, so how could they do otherwise?

In contrast to the mere ability to make promises, Nietzsche is interested in the right to make promises. What might that mean in this context? Someone with the right to make promises is someone who can fulfill the obligation without the supporting scaffold of morality. This is someone who can, through his or her own power, guarantee the future. Such a person would be a "sovereign individual." The sovereign individual is someone "beyond good and evil," no longer beholden to the values of our current morality. The sovereign individual does not simply assume that the current values are valuable but creates his or her own values. The sovereign individual does not ask, "How *should* we live?" He asks, "How *might* we live?" (II, §2).

The sovereign individual is Nietzsche's hope for the future. It is his hope that the overcoming of our current values might produce someone with the right to make promises. Here we see very clearly that Nietzsche is not arguing for a return to the old morality. We cannot turn the Chihuahua back into a wolf. The future lies in creating something new, not in rehashing the old. However, the new must be created from the materials at hand. The sovereign individual is the fruit of the new morality. The sovereign individual is what might make our long detour through weakness and resentment worthwhile. There are, of course, no guarantees that the sovereign individual will arise from the ruins of the current morality. The only thing Nietzsche does know is that all value systems eventually come to an end, crushed by their own weight. In light of this, Nietzsche can only hope that the future might produce a stronger, healthier individual (II, §2).

Debtors and creditors

Despite this brief glimpse into what lies beyond good and evil, it is not clear at all what any of this has to do with the moral terms under evaluation here, "guilt" and "bad conscience." The key, as it turns out, is Nietzsche's discussion of promising. We obviously find the need to make and keep promises in numerous contexts, but perhaps the most important and longstanding of these is in an economic context. People make promises when they are buying and selling. A farmer promises to repay a rancher for an ox that he needs to plow his fields when the harvest comes. Until he is able to repay, the farmer is in debt to the rancher. What Nietzsche finds fascinating about this circular relation of debt and repayment set in motion by promises is that the German word for "debts" (*Schulden*) is clearly related to the German word for "guilt" (*Schuld*). The connection between debt and guilt suggests a genealogical problem that Nietzsche spends the rest of the essay solving: namely, How did the mundane economic concept of debt become the fraught psychological and theological concept of guilt? Upon solving this problem, Nietzsche can turn to the evaluative question: Has the transformation of debt into guilt been a healthy or unhealthy development (II, §4)?

In order to uncover the transformation of debt into guilt Nietzsche examines the relation between creditor and debtor. He is much more interested in the times when it breaks down rather than when it functions smoothly. What happens when the farmer cannot repay the rancher? What if the crops fail and all his labor is lost? He still owes the rancher for the price of the ox. If he cannot pay what he owes, he can only give himself to the rancher, who is now able to "inflict every kind of indignity and torture upon the body of the debtor" (II, §5). Such behavior today would rightly be called criminal and is seen only in popular conceptions of loan sharks, but for Nietzsche it has its roots in the most ancient laws. The real question, though, is How does this "economy" work? How did discharging debts for cruelty become a law? Such an "economy" works only if the creditor actually receives something in the exchange. Instead of money, the creditor receives pleasure, "the pleasure of being allowed to vent his power freely upon one who is powerless" (II, §5).

Nietzsche is emphatic that taking pleasure in cruelty is part of human nature. It is part of human nature because it is part of animal nature. We can see it in the way that cats toy with their prey before killing it. We can see it in the way that orcas play with seals before killing them. We can see it in the glee that children take in teasing one another. Instead of owning up to our cruelty, we have attempted to relegate it to a barbaric past through a revolution in values. The problem is that suppressing these instincts does not eliminate them. It simply means that we turn the cruelty on ourselves instead of others. The internalization of cruelty is the origin of bad conscience (II, §6).

Bad conscience and the soul

Bad conscience is the result of being cruel to ourselves. We berate ourselves when we violate the values of the new morality. Why? What do we gain by being cruel to ourselves? The answer is the same for us as it was for the rancher. Our reward is pleasure. We take pleasure in having mastery over ourselves. There is some small part of us that enjoys the feeling of belittling someone weaker than us. In this case, though, we are also the weaker person. Bad conscience is the internalization of the creditor/debtor relationship. We are both creditor and debtor to ourselves. The "economy" functions exactly the same. It is kept in motion by the pleasure we take in cruelty (II, §16).

Bad conscience is not the only consequence of suppressing our instincts. Nietzsche also claims that we can find the origins of our soul here. This is a strange and radical claim and differs wildly from the other philosophers that we have read. For all of the other philosophers, "being human" and "having a soul" were equivalent expressions, even if they might quibble about the nature of the soul. Nietzsche not only is claiming that "being human" does not entail "having a soul;" he is suggesting that the development of a soul may not have been entirely salutary (II, §16).

Nietzsche's genealogy of the soul begins with civilization. In order for humans to live in a society, it is imperative that they not act on their instincts. This creates two problems. First, it is really hard to not act on instinct. Instincts are what allow us to act quickly, with certainty, and without deliberation. We do not second-guess instincts. We do not even first-guess instincts. We act on them without reflection. Intervening in this process is difficult and requires a system of laws and punishments to continually remind us not to act on our instincts. For example, when faced with hostility, biochemical processes prepare my body to flee or fight. In a society, though, neither of these instinctual responses is wholly viable. I cannot start whaling on someone who cuts in front of me at Starbucks. While walking away is slightly more plausible, it results in me not getting any coffee. The most likely result is that I will stew in my anger and content myself with some sort of imaginary revenge, such as envisioning the person who cut in front of me spilling his coffee on the way out the door (II, §16).

The second problem with not acting on our instincts is that our instincts are replaced by our consciousness. Instead of automatically knowing what to do, we now have to think about *everything* we do. Nietzsche imagines at first that replacing instinct with deliberation must have been miserable. He likens it to sea creatures becoming land creatures. In the sea, the water supported their weight. Movement was effortless and graceful. On land, the movements that once propelled them were difficult and awkward. Here we can compare a seal's movements in water to its movements on land. In the same way, where once our actions were immediate and fluid, they are now fraught. Every action must now be deliberated about, picked at, rehearsed, and reflected on once it is over. Did I do the right thing? Did I follow the law? Were my actions "good"? The certainty of our instincts is replaced by our weak and vacillating consciousness when we begin living in society (II, §16).

Replacing instinct with consciousness had the consequence of creating an interior life rather than a purely external one. By "interior life," Nietzsche means that we began developing an interior dialogue with ourselves. We began to question ourselves about our motives and actions. What should I do? What will the consequences of this action be? Is this right? What will others think if I do this? With questions like these we are suddenly caught in a web of deliberation. We begin placing greater and greater value on the ability to deliberate. As a result, we nurture and encourage this interior life, and it begins to grow. As it takes on greater importance, our interior life displaces instinct as the wellspring of our actions. We begin to think it is the most important part of who we are. We may even begin to think that it is immortal, since it is so distinct from our animal, bodily nature. Thus, the soul is born (II, §16).

Notice that, as with morality, the birth of the soul is the result of the shifting application of power. Society requires that instincts be contained. As contained, though, they do not simply disappear. They are turned inward. This shift from an exterior, immediate, instinctive life to an interior, mediated, reflective life becomes the soul. The soul becomes the place where formerly outwardly discharged instincts are contained and prevented from discharging outwardly. Society in turn reinforces this internalization of the instincts by creating institutions that extol the life of the soul. Chief among these institutions is religion (II, §16).

Guilt and religion

Nietzsche's genealogy of the soul shows how the economic concept of debt becomes the *psychological* concept of bad conscience. His genealogy of religion shows how the economic concept of debt becomes the *theological* concept of guilt. By separating out the genealogies of guilt and bad conscience Nietzsche is not arguing that they are fundamentally different. Rather, the purpose of the different genealogies is to account for the different valences of each concept. As we have seen, bad conscience suggests an interior and reflexive relation. While guilt also requires interiority and reflection, there is an unmistakable social component that has legal and religious implications. In short, bad conscience leans heavily on one's self-relation, whereas guilt points more towards one's social relations (II, §8).

What do we owe to society? Notice that the very way that the question is framed connects economics and society. Of course, though we sometimes owe society money in the form of taxes, most of our obligations to society take the more abstract form of obeying laws and voting. Nietzsche is interested in the origins of our obligations to society. He imagines that early societies were fragile and could little tolerate any lawlessness. In early societies, the punishment for breaking the law was banishment or death. As a society became stronger, though, it could better tolerate lawlessness. One lawless act was no longer a threat to the foundations of society. Minor infractions could be more easily overlooked. What might we owe to a society such as this (II, §10)?

Nietzsche contends that the more powerful a society becomes, the more we owe it. The more powerful a society is, the more it is able to provide for its members. The more it is able to provide for its members, the more its members owe it in return. For Nietzsche, the relationship between society and the individual is nothing other than the creditor/debtor relation writ large. The individual must pay what is owed to society. If the individual does not live up to his obligations, he must face society's punishment. The pain inflicted on the individual through punishment is sufficient to maintain the economy of individual and society (II, §10).

In addition to individual debt increasing as the power of society increases, religion also begins to take shape. Religion begins in the veneration of one's ancestors. The debt one owes to society gets transferred to the founders of society. Rituals develop around honoring the founders. Transgressions are characterized as an affront to the ancestors, and atonement for transgressions is also ritualized. Obviously, there must be a class of people who ensure that all of these rituals are properly carried out and to interpret the will of the ancestors. This requires the development of a priestly class whose hold on power is directly tied to the flourishing of society (II, §19).

As the power of a society increases, so does regard for the founders. A powerful society must have had very powerful ancestors indeed. A society might even begin to venerate such powerful ancestors as more than human. Thus, the gods are born. The historical example that is probably informing Nietzsche's genealogy of religion here is Ancient Rome. As Rome began to reflect on and mythologize its origins, the stories surrounding Romulus, the founder, take on increasing importance. Ultimately, Rome's sacred mission is secured by turning Romulus into a god (II, §19).

If regard for the founders of society leads to deification of the founders, then the power imputed to the gods increases as the power of society increases. Importantly, as the power of society increases, so does the debt owed to it. At this point, however, the debt is no longer owed to society but to the gods. Here we have the shift from debt as an economic concept to guilt as a theological concept, a debt owed to the gods. As the power of the gods increases, one's ability to repay it decreases. One finds oneself with a debt that can only be repaid with great sacrifice, if at all (II, §20).

How much would we owe to an infinite and infinitely powerful God? What would we owe to an omnipotent, omniscient, omnipresent God, who creates and sustains all things? Our debt to an infinite God would itself be infinite. The debt that cannot be repaid, the debt around which life is organized, the debt owed to an infinite God is guilt. While indebtedness to society begins as a communal and economic relation, it culminates in Christian Europe in a theological relation of infinite guilt, the debt that can never be repaid (II, §21).

At least, the debt can never be repaid by us. However, and this is what Nietzsche calls "that stroke of genius on the part of Christianity," it is possible for God to repay the debt.

> God himself sacrifices himself for the guilt of mankind, God himself makes payment to himself, God as the being who can redeem man from what has become unredeemable for man himself – the creditor sacrifices himself for his debtor, out of love (can one credit that?), out of love for his debtor! – (*Genealogy* II, §21)

For Nietzsche, there is a real tragedy here. Through our social and theological obligations, we have convinced ourselves that we are despicable and worthless to such a degree that we can never overcome it. Christianity "solves" this problem through the story of Jesus' sacrifice, but only at the price of maintaining our fundamental unworthiness. We can never earn redemption; it is a gift of grace. Nietzsche is astonished that we could hate ourselves so much as to require a salvation like that (II, §§21-2).

For Nietzsche, then, guilt and bad conscience are the long story of the way that we have mangled ourselves out of self-hatred. We have engaged in a breeding program that selects for the traits of resentment and self-hatred in an effort to promulgate a particular idea of the "good." To be sure, there is an expression of power here, but it is an expression of power that refuses to acknowledge itself as power. The new morality hides its power behind ideals of unselfishness and equality, but these are nothing other than a sign that sickness is now mistaken for health, that weakness is now mistaken for strength. It is a sign that, through cleverness, the hatred of humanity has replaced the love of humanity as an ideal. Our breeding program has turned wolves into Chihuahuas and now holds up Chihuahuas as the goal. Nietzsche's hope is that we might overcome our current values. We have changed ourselves too much to turn back into wolves, but what might we become beyond our current values?

Summary

In the Second Essay of the *Genealogy*, Nietzsche takes up the origin of the moral terms "guilt" and "bad conscience." He argues that these psychological and theological terms have their origin in economic debt and the individual's relation to society. In the individual's relation to society we also discover the origins of religion and the soul.

Questions

1. Are all values the expression of power?
2. Is the soul the result of living in society?
3. Is religion the result of our self-hatred?

11

Levinas: Philosophy and Appropriation
("Ethics as First Philosophy")

Key terms

Appropriation – Making the other the same. Taking ownership of something that is not mine.
Wisdom – That which lies beyond traditional philosophy.
Ethics – A non-appropriating relation to the other.
Intentionality – The appropriating relation between consciousness and its object.
Knowledge – The appropriating relation between knower and known.

All philosophy is characterized by its critical stance with regard to what preceded it. With Nietzsche, however, we saw this tendency taken to an extreme, especially in his willingness to call into question the relation between reason and morality. The attack on reason does not begin with Nietzsche. There is a long line of thinkers in religion and mysticism that question the authority of reason. What is new in Nietzsche is the systematic way in which he uncovers the role of power lying behind all of our most revered institutions. Nietzsche's conclusion is that the use of reason and morality is a ploy by the weak to control the strong. Levinas takes a similarly broad view of the history of philosophy. He thinks that, despite the great variety among philosophies, there is a basic structure that is constitutive of philosophical thought. However, in sharp contrast with Nietzsche, Levinas does not think that the basic structure of philosophy represents a victory of the weak over the strong. On the contrary, Levinas thinks that the very structure of philosophy is itself violent and oppressive. Far from being emblematic of the victory of the weak, philosophy is the long history of excluding the weak and helpless. What Levinas proposes is a rethinking of philosophy from the ground up. For Levinas, philosophy no longer begins with basic questions about the nature of reality, what we called "metaphysics" in Aristotle and Spinoza. Rather, philosophy begins with the face-to-face ethical relation. This is why his essay is entitled, "Ethics as *First* Philosophy."

Since Levinas is calling into question the very foundations of Western thought, we can see that his work best answers the question How might we live? Though his answer will differ profoundly from Nietzsche's, Levinas is still trying to think through what philosophy might mean beyond the longstanding structures of Western thought. He is looking for a "beyond" or what is "other" than traditional thought. As a result, his philosophy does not neatly answer Aristotle and Spinoza's How should we live? or Kant and Mill's How should we act? Rather his analysis wants to expose what these very questions presuppose. Crucially, though, Levinas's analysis does not depend on the same methodology as Nietzsche's. As we will see, this difference in methodology will lead Levinas to a very different place. His criticisms are no less devastating, and his conclusions are no less radical for this shift in methodology.

The basic structure of Western philosophy

Levinas's writing is admittedly difficult. Part of its difficulty lies in the fact that it assumes a great deal about the history of philosophy, particularly twentieth-century German philosophy. We will use the philosophy we have already read in order to clarify Levinas's claims. The first part of Levinas's argument claims that, despite superficial differences, all Western philosophy has the same basic starting point. That starting point is a structure that relates self and world, or subject and object. The terms of the relation change, depending on the philosophy, but the basic idea is that philosophy begins in the confrontation of one who seeks knowledge with the object of knowledge. Here we can think in the most basic categories. I look around my desk and I can immediately identify several objects: "computer," "keyboard," "pen," "notebook," etc. I, the knower, am connected to objects, the known, through a relation called "knowledge." We can schematize the basic structure of Western thought this way:

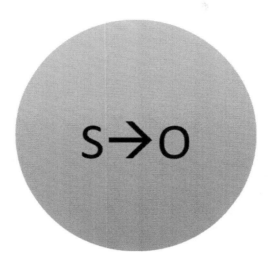

Here "S" stands for "subject" and "O" stands for "object." The arrow signifies the relation between subject and object, what may be called "knowledge" (76).[1]

What really interests Levinas here is the nature of the relation between S and O. This does not mean that Levinas is interested in knowledge *per se*. Levinas is not interested in epistemology, a theory of knowledge, but ontology or metaphysics, claims about the basic nature of reality. His question is not, What is knowledge? His question is What unacknowledged assumptions make it possible to call that relation "knowledge" in the first place? To construe the world and our

---

[1] There is, at this point, no standard edition of Levinas's work in French or English. Thus, I will refer to pagination from Seán Hand's translation of "Ethics as First Philosophy" in *The Levinas Reader*.

place in it as a knowing subject related to an object of knowledge is already to construe the knowledge as appropriation (76).

"Appropriation" is not a word we use very often. We might hear it used in a political context to talk about the "appropriation of funds," or we might hear it used in a legal context in the phrase "misappropriation of funds." In both instances, "appropriation" has the sense of "getting" or "receiving." This is certainly on the right track, but we will benefit further if we think about the root word. The root word of "appropriation" (*proprium*) is the same root as for words such as "proper" and "property." When I appropriate something, it belongs to me. It is my property. It is properly mine (76).

Thus, when Levinas claims that the relation between subject and object is a relation of appropriation, he is claiming that, through knowing, we make the object of our knowledge proper to us, our property. Levinas is not saying that, when we look at someone else's car and recognize it as a Honda, it magically becomes our car. What he is saying, though, is that, in the movement of an object from unknown to known, it does become "ours" in a conceptual sense. Think, for example, about the philosophers we have read about in this book. Initially, each philosopher was opaque and difficult to understand, unknown. Gradually, however, we were able to connect what each philosopher said with things that we already knew. "Oh, so Aristotle is saying that moderation is the key to the good life. Now, I get it." That moment of insight is the moment that Aristotle became ours. We appropriated Aristotle (76).

Obviously, different philosophers will have very different ideas about how we move from the unknown to the known. Plato thinks that the process is a kind of remembering. Aristotle thinks it occurs through definition. Spinoza thinks it happens by seeing the necessity of things. Others think it happens through the input of our senses. More recent philosophers think it happens through language. Levinas is not offering a new theory of knowledge that competes with these theories. He is interested in what they all have in common. What they all have in common is that, regardless of the nature of the process, the process itself is always a process of appropriation by which the unknown becomes mine (76).

What's wrong with appropriation?

According to Levinas, the way we come to know things is a process of appropriation. What exactly is Levinas's objection, though? Why is this a bad thing? Is it not good to learn things? It is certainly the case that the dominant trend in philosophy has emphasized the value of knowledge and the harm of ignorance. Even Nietzsche, who has sharp criticisms of the tradition, is still trying to teach us something. Is Levinas not also trying to teach us something here? How can he say it is bad? It would be difficult for Levinas to maintain that we simply abandon the project of knowledge and live in blinkered ignorance. He does, however, think that the process of appropriation is not wholly innocent (85).

The problem with appropriation becomes clearer if we think a little more about what knowing entails. The fact is that none of our knowledge is immediate. Our knowledge is not simply a reflection of the world around us. Our knowing is active and processes what we know. Let's look at a couple of basic examples of this processing. In order to see anything we need light. Our eyes and our entire visual apparatus, however, have evolved to see only certain wavelengths of light, known as the "visible spectrum." Above (ultraviolet) or below (infrared) this spectrum is "light" that is not visible. Our vision of anything is thus already a selection of what is visible within a range of light wavelengths. When we appropriate an object of perception we mold it to our visual apparatus. Humans also have a tendency to see patterns or "wholes." If someone asks me what I see when I look out the window, I respond in terms of wholes. "I see mountains and trees, buildings and cars." I don't say, "I see a gutter, a chimney, a tire, an antenna," and then "add" these up to "a building" and "a car." This tendency to organize our perceptions into wholes means that, again, our knowing is selective and shapes the known.

This does not quite solve our problem, though. The selective nature of our knowing and the fact that our knowing shapes the known seem generally beneficial. Obviously, there are times when we overlook things because of this tendency, but by and large it seems to ensure that we are not overwhelmed with unhelpful data. What exactly is the problem here? The problem becomes clearer when we begin to think about the way the process of appropriation treats other people. The fact of the matter is that, rather than treating most people as individuals, we lump them into preexisting categories. For example, I will occasionally run into my students at the grocery store. This is an awkward situation for everyone involved. I do not know what to say to the students, and the students do not know what to say to me. After a few forced pleasantries, we quickly go on our separate ways and hope we do not run into one another in a different aisle. Part of the problem here is that neither of us sees the other as an individual. I reduce the students to the category of "student," and they reduce me to the category of "professor." When we see each other outside the context of the classroom, we do not know how to relate to one another. In this case, the appropriation that goes on is reductive, and here we can begin to see the problem with appropriation (82–3).

The problem with appropriation becomes much more apparent when we move from social awkwardness to racism and sexism. Both racism and sexism entail subsuming an individual under a preexisting category. In this case, the category "black" or "woman" tells me everything I need to know about the person. It is here that we can see the violence and oppression caused by appropriation. We are probably more likely to call this "stereotyping" than "appropriation," but Levinas's analysis here allows him to make a larger point. We tend to think of stereotyping as an individual failing. That is, when an individual makes a claim such as "all black people do X," it is easy to chalk this up to individual ignorance. Levinas's point is that appropriation is systematic. It is not an individual moral failing, but the way thought has been conceived in the West for the past 2,500 years. Appropriation is not a rare aberration, but our everyday way of being in the world. Furthermore, appropriation is so natural, so automatic, that we do not see its effects. As a result, we can unconsciously facilitate institutional racism or sexism without having any personal or conscious animosity. While racism and sexism provide clear examples of the dangers of appropriation, ultimately Levinas's concern is the way we treat other people, regardless of race or gender. If appropriation is the structure of thought itself, we are doomed to force everyone we meet into our preexisting categories. What if another way of thinking were possible?

Beyond appropriation

Levinas articulates this possibility at the beginning of the second section. He writes, "In this essay we wish to ask whether thought understood as knowledge ... has exhausted the possible modes of meaning for thought, and whether ... a more urgent form does not emerge, that of wisdom" (78). What Levinas thus intends to argue is that the basic structure of Western thought pictured above does not tell the whole story. There is more to thought than the relation of appropriation. At this point, he simply calls what lies beyond appropriation "wisdom." We can picture Levinas's claim this way:

Levinas's claim is both radical and straightforward. Previously, philosophy had defined knowledge and, along with it, wisdom as wholly contained in the appropriating relation between subject and object.

Here Levinas suggests that not only is wisdom different from knowledge, but also that wisdom itself lies beyond philosophy's reach. On this reading, philosophy has never been the "love of wisdom" but the active suppression of wisdom. Ironically, by assuming that thought naturally appropriates, philosophy has lost what it most sought, and it is only by pursuing the possibility of a "non-appropriating" relation that philosophy can find itself again (78).

In order to pursue his argument, Levinas narrows his focus to the concept of "intentionality" in a school of thought known as "phenomenology." There are several reasons for this choice. First, phenomenology was the dominant method of philosophy in Europe for the entirety of the twentieth century. Second, Levinas himself was one of the first people to introduce phenomenology to France. In essence, he is turning the phenomenological method against itself to demonstrate his point. Third, in an essay this short he cannot possibly cover the entire history of philosophy, so he focuses on one of its important and recent highlights (78–9).

Before we can follow Levinas's argument any farther, though, we need to know a little bit more about phenomenology and intentionality. Phenomenology has its origins in the early twentieth century with a German philosopher named Edmund Husserl. Husserl is trying to give an account of human experience, when he hits upon two great insights. First, human experience is conscious experience. That is, all of our experiences are the relation of human consciousness to the objects of consciousness. Or, to put the insight negatively, "unconscious experience" is an impossible contradiction in terms. Second, consciousness relates to the objects of experience "intentionally." That is, consciousness "directs itself toward" or "intends toward" its objects. Consciousness is always "consciousness of." Thus, the relation between consciousness and its objects is called "intentionality" (78–9).

The conclusion that Levinas draws from Husserl's insights is that phenomenology has the same structure as the rest of Western philosophy. Phenomenology posits a knowing subject that appropriates the known. The only notable difference, as far as Levinas is concerned, is that Husserl renames the appropriating relationship "intentionality." Within this context, Levinas asks the basic question of phenomenology, Does intentionality fully account for human experience? However, notice that Levinas is turning the basic question of phenomenology against phenomenology. He does not want to assume that all experience is already intentional. He wants to know if something lies outside of intentionality, what he calls the "non-intentional." This is nothing other than the "wisdom" of the above diagram. We can present Levinas's equivalences as a diagram here:

Wisdom = Non-Appropriating = Non-Intentional

In order to uncover whether something like a non-intentional consciousness is possible, Levinas will examine the experience of aging (79).

Aging

It is undeniable that we are continuously aging, but what is our experience of aging? Here the question becomes much more difficult. Is aging an object of consciousness? Can I see myself aging? Can I sit in front of a mirror and watch myself getting older? No. Even though aging happens continuously, its effects are too gradual to be seen. My parents ask me every year on my birthday if I feel any older. I have been asked this dozens of time in my life, yet, despite being demonstrably older, I never do feel any older. I can see that I am older when I look at old photographs. I can see that my family is getting older and can only assume that I am aging at the same rate, but I never actually see or feel myself getting older (79).

If aging is an experience, it seems really different from our other experiences. When I see clouds or hear birds outside my window, these are clear experiences with defined objects. With aging, something is happening to me, but neither the source nor the effects are clear (at least immediately). When I look outside, I actively perceive the objects of experience. Aging happens to me. I am wholly passive with regard to aging. There is nothing I can do to stop it or slow it down. It is inexorable. Every second that passes makes me just a little bit older (80).

The strangeness of the experience of aging brings phenomenology to an impasse. Everyone agrees that aging differs from other kinds of experience. Either one must argue that, despite its strangeness, aging can still be appropriated by intentionality, or one must argue that aging lies outside of intentionality and points to the limits of phenomenology specifically and philosophy generally. Traditional phenomenology attempts to argue that aging can, in fact, be an object of intentional consciousness. Levinas argues that it cannot (80–1).

In order to illustrate the difference between these two positions, let's take a brief detour through Freud. For Freud, there are three levels to our mental capacities: conscious, preconscious, and unconscious. The conscious level contains things that we are currently aware of. I am right now conscious of my hands on the keyboard and the computer screen in front of me. The preconscious level contains things that I am not now aware of, but could be made aware. I am not currently aware of the name of my second-grade teacher or my home address when I was in second grade, but this is information that could be dredged up, should it be needed. The unconscious level, for Freud, contains those drives that I can never be directly aware of, the life and death drives. Or, if we wanted a more contemporary analog, I do not have access to my brain's electro-chemical functioning. I simply do not have the perceptual apparatus that would allow me to see (let alone control) the release of neurotransmitters in my brain.[2]

With this illustration in mind, we can see where Levinas stands in relation to traditional phenomenology. Levinas is arguing that aging is "unconscious" insofar as it cannot, in principle, be made conscious. Traditional phenomenology argues that aging is "preconscious" in that, while it is not normally conscious, it can, in principle, be made conscious. If Levinas is right about aging, then he has discovered something beyond the intentional, a non-intentional consciousness that would shake the very foundations of philosophy (81).

How can he prove this, though? In some respects Levinas is in the same boat as Nietzsche. Both are trying to talk about what lies "beyond," but both are limited to the vocabulary of the here and now. Levinas is in the unenviable position of talking about what lies beyond philosophy using the language of philosophy. With respect to aging, he looks at the attempts of traditional phenomenology to show that it can be an object of intentional consciousness. Levinas notes that while traditional phenomenology does not speak about aging directly, it does speak about the passage of time as a "pure duration."

---

[2] Sigmund Freud, *The Interpretation of Dreams*, SE V:594.

> This duration remains free from the sway of the will, absolutely outside all activity of the ego, and exactly like the ageing process which is probably the perfect model of passive synthesis, a lapse of time no act of remembrance, reconstructing the past, could possibly reverse. (80–1)

To Levinas it looks as if traditional phenomenology wants to have it both ways. On the one hand, it recognizes that our experience of movement through time (duration/aging) is passive. Such a passage does not involve anything like a will or activity on our part. On the other hand, despite having characteristics that directly oppose intentionality at every point, traditional phenomenology still wants to claim that duration/aging could be made an object of intentional consciousness (81).

Levinas is not buying it. He agrees with traditional phenomenology's analysis of aging/duration, but thinks the continued insistence that such a phenomenon could ever be intentional is misguided. Phenomenology's failure to examine its own presuppositions has led to a failure in accounting for human experience. A more rigorous phenomenology would recognize this and acknowledge that aging cannot be subsumed by intentionality. "Does not the temporality of implicit time . . . here signify otherwise than as knowledge taken on the run, otherwise than a way representing presence or the non-presence of the future and the past?" (81). Aging signifies otherwise; it points beyond the bounds of traditional philosophy. It forces us to rebuild philosophy on a very different foundation.

The reserve of the stranger

It is admittedly difficult to see how something as commonplace as aging leads to the unraveling of Western philosophy. As we have seen, though, Levinas accomplishes this by going after the basic structure of Western philosophy rather than each philosophy individually. What remains to be seen are the implications of the non-intentional. Here Levinas introduces many of the themes that will occupy him for the remainder of the essay. "This implication of the non-intentional is a form of *mauvaise conscience*; it has no intentions, or aims, and cannot avail itself of the protective mask of a character contemplating in the mirror of the world a reassured and self-positing portrait" (81).

The non-intentional must, by definition, be the opposite of everything the intentional consciousness is. It is naked and powerless, exposed. Levinas says it is "a form of *mauvaise conscience.*" This can be translated as either "bad consciousness" or "bad conscience." Both are apt. Translating as "bad consciousness" makes a clear connection between traditional phenomenology's intentional consciousness as "good" consciousness and Levinas's non-intentional consciousness as "bad" consciousness. At the same time, translating as "conscience" invokes the ethical direction that Levinas intends to take the discussion. Furthermore, "bad conscience" evokes Nietzsche's discussion from the previous chapter. Crucially, though, while Nietzsche argued that bad conscience is a historically produced sign of sickness, Levinas will argue that bad conscience is foundational to who we are as humans, but that it has been obscured by our insistence on "good conscience" (81).

Levinas continues, "This is either *mauvaise conscience* or timidity; it is not guilty but accused; and responsible for its very presence. It has not yet been invested with any attributes or justified in any way. This creates the reserve of the stranger" (81). We will return to the themes of accusation, responsibility, and justification in the next chapter. To conclude this chapter, I would like to focus on what it means for *mauvaise conscience* to create the reserve of the stranger. When we think of the word "reserve," the first thing that probably comes to mind is an "animal reserve." An animal reserve is a sanctuary where animals can be safe from predation and human encroachment. I think Levinas is using "reserve" in exactly this sense. Non-intentional consciousness creates a safe space. In this case, however, the safe space is for the stranger.

In order to see why Levinas uses "stranger" here, let's do a thought experiment. If appropriating, intentional consciousness is all that exists, is it possible to meet a stranger? If thinking works solely by making the unknown known, do strangers even exist? Well, what makes a stranger a stranger is being unknown. As soon as the stranger is known, she is no longer a stranger. Traditional philosophy works by making the unknown known, so it looks as if it would be impossible to meet a stranger. There is no place in traditional philosophy for the unknown to remain unknown. There is no reserve of the stranger in traditional philosophy. It is only if something lies outside the traditional that there can be a reserve of the stranger (81).

We can see the importance of the reserve of the stranger if we think back to our discussion of stereotypes. Stereotypes are damaging because they force people into preexisting categories. If appropriation is the only way we can think, then we are forever doomed to eliminate the difference and otherness of people we encounter. We will only ever meet versions of ourselves. Non-intentional consciousness, *mauvaise conscience*, at least makes it possible to relate to others in a different way, a way that does not subsume them into our preexisting categories. For Levinas, only a non-appropriating relation can be ethical because it is the only kind of relation that does not do violence to the other. It is the only kind of relation that can meet the other as other; it is the only kind of relation that can create a reserve of the stranger.

Summary

Levinas argues that the history of Western thought has been the history of appropriation. He proposes that appropriation does not tell the whole story, though. He argues that aging suggests the possibility of a relation that lies outside of appropriation and thus makes possible a non-appropriating ethical relation that is the true foundation of thought.

Questions

1. What is wrong with appropriation?
2. How would avoiding appropriation be ethical?
3. Can you compare Levinas's good and bad conscience with Nietzsche's good and bad conscience?

12

Levinas: Ethics and the Other
("Ethics as First Philosophy")

Key terms

Other – That which lies outside appropriation.
Justification – The problem of existence. How can we justify ourselves if others are suffering?
Face – The literal face of the other person. That which calls us to justify our existence.
Asymmetry – In the ethical relation obligation only flows to the other. Ethics does not presuppose reciprocity.

In his play *No Exit*, Jean-Paul Sartre, Levinas's contemporary, famously claims, "Hell is other people." It would be easy to read this quote as a rallying cry for a kind of radical individualism, and, indeed, it is often read this way. However, Sartre, commenting on the play much later, claims that the meaning was much more subtle. The problem is not that our sole source of misery is interacting with other people. The problem is that we necessarily depend on others to understand ourselves. We come to understand ourselves in the way that others become a mirror of self-knowledge. Although Sartre's direct inspiration for this idea came from phenomenology and the philosophy of nineteenth-century German philosopher G. W. F. Hegel, we can see this idea already at work in Plato and Aristotle. As we saw, education was so important for Aristotle because the praise or blame of others shapes who we are. If this praise or blame is misguided, we will fail in our quest to live the best kind of life. This failure will be rooted in the fact that we misunderstand ourselves. Misunderstanding ourselves because others reflect us in a distorted way is why other people can be hell for Sartre.[1]

Sartre's position thus expresses the longstanding way the tradition has taken up the problem of other people in philosophy. Obviously, philosophy has a great deal to say about the role of other people in everyday life. Other people are crucial for our self-formation. We are fundamentally social creatures. Thus living well and acting rightly surely involves doing this in the context of other people. As Mill argues, the principle that determines right action is the one that seeks the happiness of the greatest number of people.

It is precisely at this point that we can see where Levinas departs from traditional views of other people. While no one we have read up to this point would deny the importance of other people, all of them subordinate other people to the more fundamental task of self-knowledge. For Levinas, though, the task of self-knowledge is simply another way in which philosophy pursues appropriation. In this case, the other person becomes a help or a hindrance to knowing oneself. The subject appropriates the object in the quest to fulfill the Delphic oracle's charge, "Know Thyself."

In contrast to this, Levinas argues that the quest for self-knowledge does not tell the whole story. His analysis of aging suggests that beyond the limits laid out by the search for knowledge lies the possibility of a non-appropriating relationship, a relationship in which the other person would not simply be a means to understanding oneself but a space in which the other person can remain other. This is the "reserve of the stranger." This relation to the other person as wholly other, as non-appropriable, not only lies outside of philosophy but is, in fact, the very ground that makes philosophy possible. This is what Levinas means by "ethics," and it is why he calls ethics "first philosophy."

First philosophy

In order to see why Levinas's claim is so radical, we need to look at the phrase "first philosophy." Since Aristotle, "first philosophy" has always referred to metaphysics, the study of what is really real. In

---

[1] Sartre, *The Writings of Jean-Paul Sartre, vol. 1: A Biographical Life*, p. 459ff.

Aristotle, metaphysics meant getting straight the form and content of things. In Spinoza, it meant understanding that everything was part of a single substance. In Nietzsche, it meant seeing the underlying power relations. Ultimately, however, all of these speculations about what is really real derive from a strange observation that Aristotle makes in the *Metaphysics*. Take the following sentences:

1. This table is brown.
2. I am free.
3. The truth is out there.
4. God is real.

All of the sentences make the claim that something "is" the case. Or, in philosophy, we would say that some property is predicated of a subject. Brownness is predicated of the table. Freedom is predicated of me. Reality is predicated of God. Aristotle is puzzled, though, by how "is" functions in each case. Does God exist in the same way that the table does? Do I exist in the same way as the truth? Aristotle thinks that the "is" functions differently in each case. While subsequent philosophy has largely agreed with him, this raises some problems. Chief among these problems is defining "is" if it functions with such variety. What can "is" even mean, if its meaning is constantly shifting? Aristotle thinks this question must be answered first before we can answer any other questions. Answering this question is the task of metaphysics. Metaphysics tells us what "is" is. This is why, traditionally, metaphysics is deemed first philosophy.[2]

Levinas argues that the result of making metaphysics first philosophy is appropriation. Despite all the differences in philosophies throughout the centuries, beginning with metaphysics continually reproduces the same underlying structure whereby the other is reduced to the same. When we begin with metaphysics, the "ethics" or "morality" that we construct in that context will simply express the quest for self-knowledge. Our relation to the other becomes the means to improving ourselves. Levinas wonders what might be possible if we did not begin with metaphysics. What if something besides

---

[2] Aristotle, *Metaphysics* Z.1, 1028a10–25.

questions about the meaning of "is" were our starting point? What if we began with a relation to the other that was not an expression of our self-knowledge? Levinas cleared the ground for this project in the opening sections of his essay by arguing for the possibility of a non-intentional consciousness. This showed that metaphysics as first philosophy did not tell the whole story. Thus, Levinas begins again, not with metaphysics but with ethics (86).

Justification

As we have seen, the idea that we are dependent on others for who we are has a long history. As with all things, philosophers dispute exactly how dependent we are on others, but Levinas will push this idea to its radical extreme. We can see the radicality of Levinas's view if we ask, Which comes first: the self or the other? The other views that argue for dependency maintain the primacy of the self. Even if the self is seen as very dependent on others, the overall project of self-knowledge ensures that, at bottom, the self is primary. In contrast to this, Levinas is not interested in the project of self-knowledge. He argues for the primacy of the other in the self/other relationship. The other is not simply a more or less necessary means to self-knowledge. For Levinas, the other actually constitutes the self (81–2).

The fact that the other is primary in the self/other relation reorients philosophy itself. Since the relation to the other replaces metaphysics as first philosophy, this means that questions about metaphysics or what "is" is must be framed differently. The traditional primacy of metaphysics meant that, even though the meaning of existence was continually questioned, the goodness of existence never was. Existence was always seen as self-justifying, a good in itself. This idea was most clearly articulated in Spinoza, who argued, as we saw, that the essence of all things is self-preservation. From Levinas's perspective, this is tantamount to assuming that existence needs no justification, since its mere preservation lies at the heart of all things. The displacement of the primacy of metaphysics now gives us a vantage point from which to ask not what "is" means, but whether existence itself is justified. We can make sense of this claim if we compare the image of traditional philosophy to Levinas's philosophy:

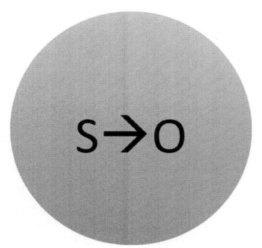

Traditional philosophy

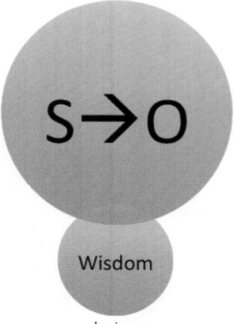

Levinas

Insofar as traditional philosophy assumes that metaphysics is first philosophy, it provides no vantage point from which to judge whether the project itself is justified. The whole project becomes circular and self-justifying. In contrast to this, Levinas's philosophy argues that there is, in fact, a vantage point from which to call philosophy itself into question. He initially calls this vantage point wisdom, but now we can see that it is the non-appropriating relation to the other, the relation in which we are constituted by the other. This is the ethical relation that calls existence into question (81–2).

The idea that existence needs justification is abstract in the extreme. What could this even mean? How would we go about doing that? Here we move from a structural argument about the entirety of Western thought to the concrete and practical. Levinas is not interested in a general theory of justification, whereby we could prove once and for all that existence is justified. Attempting a justification on this level would simply repeat the traditional structure of thought. No, this justification and the need for it are intensely personal. The question is not How can existence justify itself? but How can *my* existence justify itself? Suddenly I find myself personally at stake in Levinas's philosophy (82).

Why am I at stake, though? What is it about my existence that requires justification? Levinas's reply is that it is nothing about your existence, nothing that you have done. You are not guilty of anything, but that does not absolve you of the need for justification. For Levinas, it is the very fact of my existence that requires justification. Even though I am not guilty of anything, the very fact of my existence means I stand accused. Accused of what? By whom? Levinas writes,

> One has to respond to one's right to be ... because of one's fear for the Other. My being-in-the-world or ... my being at home, have these not also been the usurpation of spaces belonging to the other man whom I have already oppressed or starved, or driven out into a third world; are they not acts of repulsing, excluding, exiling, stripping, killing? (82)

This is beginning to sound like a movie, where I am accused of a crime I did not commit. It is difficult to see what's ethical about this.

Let's follow Levinas's reasoning here. My existence requires justification because the bare fact of my existence entails the exclusion of others. The fact that I am simply *here* in this place means that no one else can be here in this place. To illustrate this with a less charged example: I have a backpack sitting on a chair in my office. If a student comes in, she cannot sit in the chair because the backpack is taking up that space. Or, if I am driving on the highway and I need to change lanes in order to exit, but I cannot because there is a car occupying the space that I need, then I am forced to speed up, slow down, or go to the next exit. In both cases, it is not as if the backpack or car are acting in a malicious way. They are not guilty of anything. At the same time, though, the very fact of their existence means that no one or no thing can occupy the space that they occupy. In the same way, being born, coming into existence, means that I occupy a place. This is the unavoidable nature of existence. The fact of my existence places an inescapable burden on me. I am responsible for those who cannot occupy the space that I occupy. This is why my existence needs justification. This is why ethics comes before metaphysics (82).

The face

How can we justify ourselves in the face of a responsibility such as this? It seems as if Levinas is approaching the kind of infinite guilt that Nietzsche was so critical of in *The Genealogy of Morals*, except that Levinas wants to use this unavoidable responsibility as the ground of thought, not something to be overcome. Levinas's claim here is not fundamentally theological. Our debt is not owed to God. Our debt is owed to the other. Furthermore, the way one justifies one's existence is not through belief but through action. The spur to action lies not in vague platitudes about helping others, but in the face of the person in front of you right now. Levinas writes, "Responsibility for the Other, for the naked face of the first individual to come along" (83).

In this regard, Levinas speaks of the "irruption of the face." "Irruption" is a strange word, but it is precisely chosen. We are much more familiar with other words with the "rupt" root, such as "rupture," "interrupt," and "eruption," so what can we make of the "ir-" prefix?

This becomes clearest if we compare "irruption" to "eruption." The first thing that comes to mind when we think of the word "eruption" is a volcano. A volcano erupts when internal forces build to the point that they can no longer be contained. These forces are then released as gas, ash, and lava, which flow out from the volcano. The crucial point here is that an "eruption" is a movement from the inside to the outside. An "irruption" moves from the outside to the inside. A group of noisy children returning from recess *irrupt* into the classroom. When class is over, they *erupt* outside. When Levinas says the face "irrupts," we should picture the face intruding into our calm and self-justifying existence and disturbing it (82–3).

What is disturbing about the irruption of the face? The appearance of the face of the other accuses us. It accuses us because, by our very existence, we are taking up space that the other cannot, and now we are forced to justify our existence. Levinas puts this very elegantly by alluding to two different stories from the Bible. In the first instance, Levinas refers to the story of the brothers, Cain and Abel, from the Hebrew Bible and writes,

> But, in its expression, in its mortality, the face before me summons me, calls for me, begs for me, as if the invisible death that must be faced by the Other, pure otherness, separated, in some way, from any whole, were my business. (83)

In the book of Genesis in the Hebrew Bible, Cain murders Abel because God prefers Abel's offerings to his. Later, God asks Cain where his brother is, to which Cain famously replies, "Am I my brother's keeper?" (Gen. 4: 9). Cain obviously thinks he is not responsible for his brother, but God's subsequent punishment shows that he is. By requiring us to justify our existence, Levinas is arguing that we are surely our brothers' keepers, but his claim is even more radical than that. Since our responsibility is to the first face and any face that appears, our obligations go well beyond and precede any familial obligations (83).

Levinas's second allusion to the Bible is to the parable of the Good Samaritan told by Jesus from the Gospel of Luke. The story itself is fairly well known. A man is beaten by robbers and left for dead on the side of the road. Two passersby, a priest and a Levite, both religious leaders, ignore him but a Samaritan rescues the injured man and pays for his recovery. Making the Samaritan into the hero of the story would have scandalized Jesus' Jewish audience. The Samaritans were considered by the Jews to be a heretical sect that was not really Jewish. The idea that religious leaders could have done the wrong thing while a questionable Samaritan did the right thing would have appalled the listeners. What is less well known about the parable, though, is what prompts its telling. Jesus tells the parable in response to a series of questions from a lawyer.

> On one occasion an expert in the law stood up to test Jesus. "Teacher," he asked, "what must I do to inherit eternal life?"
>
> "What is written in the Law?" he replied. "How do you read it?"
>
> He answered, "'Love the Lord your God with all your heart and with all your soul and with all your strength and with all your mind'; and, 'Love your neighbor as yourself.'"
>
> "You have answered correctly," Jesus replied. "Do this and you will live."
>
> But he wanted to justify himself, so he asked Jesus, "And who is my neighbor?"[3]

The entire parable is in response to the question, "Who is my neighbor?" Only the Samaritan was a neighbor to the injured man, and he was a neighbor regardless of the cultural and religious beliefs that may have ordinarily separated him from the injured man. For Levinas, our neighbor is the first face to appear. Furthermore, the first face to appear is our neighbor regardless of and prior to any differences, whether ethnic, religious, or social, that we might use to shield ourselves from this obligation. Levinas calls this obligation that is thrust on us by the mere appearance of the face "A guiltless responsibility, whereby I am none the less open to an accusation of which no alibi, spatial or temporal, could clear me" (83). The priest and the Levite shut themselves off from the call of the other, but the Samaritan answered the call of the other.

---

[3] Luke 10: 25–9.

Asymmetry

It is tempting at this point to assume a kind of equality between the other and me. I think that if I am obligated to the other, then the other is just as obligated to me. Otherwise, would the relation not be unfair and therefore unethical? Levinas would say that this assumption fundamentally misunderstands the nature of the ethical relation that he is pursuing here. For Levinas, we may not assume symmetry or reciprocity in the ethical relation. The reason for this follows from the very nature of the ethical relation. Recall that what opens us to the call of the other is not a rational, universal principle that we are subject to and equal before. What opens us to the call of the other is precisely that which lies outside of the rational, active, appropriating subject. Our openness lies in a profound passivity that can never be converted into an activity of the mind or an act of will. For Levinas, the existence of such a passivity is signaled by the aging process with regard to which we are utterly passive. Insofar as the ethical relation arises from this passivity in the irruption of the face, we cannot assert our "right" to equality without destroying it. Demanding a "right" to equality in the ethical relation returns us to the assumption that our existence does not need to be justified (83–4).

We can return to the parable of the Good Samaritan to illustrate further Levinas's point. When the Good Samaritan finds the injured man on the side of the road, he cleans and bandages his wounds and then takes him on a donkey to the nearest inn. At the inn he pays the innkeeper to look after the injured man and promises to repay any additional expenses incurred upon his return. Obviously, this is a parable not a novella, so there are a lot of details that we might wish to know. We do not know how long the injured man stays at the inn. We do not know if the injured man was at the inn when the Good Samaritan returned. We do not know if the injured man ever learned the Good Samaritan's name or, for that matter, if the Good Samaritan knew the injured man's name. Did the injured man travel to Samaria to thank the Good Samaritan and offer to repay the debt? We do not know but does it matter? It certainly does not matter for the purposes of the parable, which makes very clear that being a neighbor has nothing to do with religious orthodoxy and everything to do with taking care of those in need. None of these "unknown" details matters for

Levinas's point either. The relation between the Good Samaritan and the injured man is completely asymmetrical. The Good Samaritan justifies his existence by helping the injured man without assuming that the injured man is required to help him in the same way (83).

Levinas summarizes the depth of this asymmetry when he writes,

> It is as if the other established a relationship or a relationship were established whose whole intensity consists in not presupposing the idea of community ... A responsibility for my neighbor, for the other man, for the stranger or sojourner ... is the responsibility of a hostage which can be carried to the point of being substituted for the other person ... (83–4)

Levinas makes two key points here. The first one is that the ethical relation does not presuppose the idea of community. This reinforces the asymmetrical nature of the ethical relation. A community is grounded in what all its members have in common. All members of a community are equally obligated to one another. The ethical relation does not depend on this equal obligation, and, in fact, exceeds it at every point. We can, again, see this clearly in the parable of the Good Samaritan. The members of the injured man's community pass him by. It is the outsider, the one with nothing in common, who helps the injured man (84).

The second key point that Levinas makes in the above passage emphasizes just how great the asymmetry is between the other and me. I am "hostage" to the other. I "substitute" myself for the other. The relation of a hostage to his captor is one of infinite subjection. The captor is completely active, and the hostage is completely passive. This passivity extends to the point that the other and I switch places. That is, I give up my place to the other and am myself excluded, driven out. Ethics for Levinas is not the facile injunction to be nice to one another, or even the ubiquitous Golden Rule to do to others as you would have them do to you. It is not the quest for excellence or self-preservation. It is not seeking the greatest good for the greatest number. It is not the conforming of one's will to reason, nor is it overcoming morality. No, ethics for Levinas is the continual task of justifying one's existence in the face of the other (84–5).

To be or not to be. Is that the question?

Levinas concludes his essay with a riff on Shakespeare's *Hamlet*. He takes the opening line of Hamlet's famous soliloquy, "To be or not to be – that is the question," and turns it on its head (*Hamlet* III, i). Is the question of "being," of "existence," of "is" really the most important question? Is there not a more pressing question, the question of ethics? The question of ethics is not Why is there something rather than nothing? or What is the meaning of being? The question of ethics is, How does existence justify itself? The answer to this question does not lie in acquiring more knowledge. The quest to acquire more knowledge simply returns us to the appropriating structure of Western thought. Not only does this quest not justify existence, but also it obscures the very need for existence to justify itself and begins by assuming that existence is self-justifying (85–6).

Existence justifies itself not in a principle, but practically and con-cretely. The justification of existence occurs on a purely personal level in my "capacity to fear injustice more than death, to prefer to suffer than to commit injustice, and to prefer that which justifies being over that which assures it" (85). This capacity lies not in our active willing but in our passive openness to the face of the other, which calls us out of our complacency and self-assurance to answer for our very existence. The face of the other signals the costliness of existence and asks us to justify the expense. Of course, it is possible to deny our obligations. We do it everyday. We refuse to make eye contact with the homeless person on the street. We divide the world into those who are like us and those who are not like us. We turn our backs on the needs of others (86).

Levinas, as a holocaust survivor, would not deny that we are capa-ble of monstrous inhumanity as well as daily, petty cruelties. Part of Levinas's project is to show the degree to which the very way that we think about the world is complicit in obscuring the face of the other. At the same time, he also wants to show that we find our human-ity not in the way that we pursue excellence or self-preservation or good will in the exercise of reason, but in the everyday experience of responding to the face of the other (85).

Summary

In non-intentional consciousness Levinas discovers the possibility of a non-appropriating relation that he calls the ethical relation. The ethical relation is characterized by our passivity and total obligation triggered by the face of the other. In light of this obligation, our task is to justify our existence.

Questions

1. Does my existence require justification?
2. How can I justify my existence?
3. How important is equality in ethics?

Conclusion: Beyond Beyond

Where do we go from here? Or is the question Where *should* we go from here? Or, perhaps, it is Where *might* we go from here? Hopefully, this book has given you the tools you need not only to distinguish among these questions but also to begin answering them for yourself. By way of conclusion, though, I would like to suggest some paths that you might follow.

In the Introduction I used the metaphor of a country to illustrate how we might think about the history of philosophy. Just as countries have successive eras organized around different ideas and questions, so too does philosophy. Furthermore, no country exists without internal and external resistance. With Nietzsche and Levinas we saw that one of the tasks of philosophy could be calling into question the very foundations of philosophy itself. This internal resistance can also take the form of very pointed questions about race, class, and gender. How has philosophy treated women? How has philosophy treated people of color? How has it treated the poor? Historically, the answers to these questions have been "not very well" or silence. Shifting philosophy away from its insular focus has been a driving force behind much recent work in the field. In many cases, however, those arguing for a new focus for philosophy have marshaled the resources provided by traditional philosophy. They find that, for example, Nietzsche's account of value formation allows them to analyze values – such as patriarchy or racial privilege – that Nietzsche himself did not. Or Spinoza's anti-essentialism allows some to criticize identity politics that produces an us versus them mentality. Of course, the important thing that is happening as philosophy continues to develop is the invention of new concepts and new modes of analysis that allow us to ask anew the questions of philosophy.

The external resistance to the kind of philosophy we have explored here comes in the form of other traditions of philosophy. Our exploration of philosophy has focused solely on the Western European tradition. It is a tradition with a rich and glorious heritage, to be sure, a heritage that rewards deep and careful study. However, every culture, every tradition has an equally complex series of competing philosophies. This is precisely because everyone needs to know how to live and how to act. These other traditions have developed differently, having faced different social and cultural pressures. They may be organized around different questions, and the resistances they face may be different. No doubt a book like this one could be written about each and every one of them. The important thing to recognize, though, is that just as the careful study of one country does not give you insight into other countries, so the study of one tradition does not give you insight into other traditions.

What it does give you, however, is a point of comparison. You started the book with only your intuitions about philosophy. These were mostly unexamined and, at times, inconsistent with one another. As you worked through the various thinkers in this tradition, though, some of your presuppositions were challenged, some supported. The goal was not to get you to "buy" one of the philosophies but give you the resources to figure out *what* you think and more importantly *why* you think that. You can now take these hard-won insights and put them to the test by comparing them to other traditions of philosophy. You may even discover that Buddhism, for example, offers a more compelling philosophy than the Western tradition presented here.

The important lesson in all of this is that philosophy is a lifetime task. Either you are acting according to settled principles and living according to established goals, or you are in the process of calling these principles and goals into question. Both possibilities are the task of philosophy, and the task is never done. We are all philosophers, whether we recognize it or not. The only question is whether we are good at it or not. Becoming a better philosopher, like all things, requires practice. The more widely you read, discuss, write, and think about these issues, the better you will get at it. The philosophers presented in this book are just the beginning of a long journey.

Suggestions for Further Reading

Ethics

Aristotle

As we saw, Aristotle's works are wide-ranging and foundational for Western thought in general. However, Aristotle has numerous works that touch directly on human behavior beyond the *Nicomachean Ethics*. He alludes directly to the *Politics* in the *Nicomachean Ethics*, and has another text called the *Eudemian Ethics*, which covers much of the same material. Readers might also be interested in Aristotle's discussions of human psychology in *On the Soul* and *Rhetoric*.

The secondary literature on Aristotle is incredibly rich. *The Cambridge Companion to Aristotle's* Nicomachean Ethics is an excellent place to take the measure of scholarly debates surrounding the text. Richard Kraut's *Aristotle on the Human Good* is a highly regarded discussion of Aristotle's work in relation to the good, while Julia Annas's *The Morality of Happiness* places the search for happiness in its larger historical context of the ancient Mediterranean world.

Spinoza

While Spinoza cannot claim the breadth of Aristotle, he has no fewer pretensions to completeness and has, perhaps, had a greater measure of success in constructing an all-encompassing system.

Spinoza wrote other works that address similar issues to his *Ethics*: namely, *The Treatise on the Emendation of the Intellect* and the *Short Treatise on God, Man, and his Well-Being*. However, his *Theological–Political Treatise* and *Letters* are probably better ways to see Spinoza apply himself to contemporary problems, particularly the relation between politics and religion.

There has been something of a renaissance in Spinoza scholarship recently. Michael Della Rocca's *Spinoza* is an excellent example of this recent scholarship. Steven Nadler's *Spinoza's Ethics: An Introduction* is very good, as is his biography of Spinoza. Jonathan Israel's *Radical Enlightenment* puts Spinoza's influence in historical context. Gilles Deleuze's *Spinoza: Practical Philosophy*, however, remains my favorite.

Morality

Kant

Like Spinoza, Kant had a very intricate system of philosophy articulated in three "Critiques": *The Critique of Pure Reason, The Critique of Practical Reason*, and *The Critique of Judgment*. Kant works out his moral theory most fully in *The Critique of Practical Reason*, but he explores the implications of this theory in works such as *The Metaphysics of Morals* and an essay entitled, "What is Enlightenment?"

After Plato and Aristotle, Kant is perhaps the most influential philosopher in the Western tradition. This is reflected in the vast secondary literature on Kant. Henry Allison's *Kant's Groundwork for the Metaphysics of Morals: A Commentary* and his *Kant's Theory of Freedom* are both excellent exemplars of this scholarship. Allen Wood's *Kantian Freedom* is also an important work in the field.

Mill

Mill's impact extends well beyond his moral philosophy. He is justly famous for his work in induction and probability, but he is perhaps even better known for his work in political philosophy, particularly *On Liberty* and *The Subjection of Women*, both of which deal with the issue of equality.

As always, *The Cambridge Companion to Mill* is an excellent place to start with Mill's work. Not only does it provide a sense of context, but also it gives an indication of where scholarship on Mill is headed. Wendy Donner's *Mill* is also an excellent resource.

Beyond

Nietzsche

Nietzsche's work ventures widely over topics such as art, science, religion, and philosophy, and his style varies as much as his topics. *Beyond Good and Evil* is an excellent book to read alongside *On the Genealogy of Morals*, as both cover many similar topics. Nietzsche's best-known work is *Thus Spoke Zarathustra*. It is challenging both stylistically and thematically, and I would only recommend reading it after having read broadly in Nietzsche's corpus.

The secondary literary on Nietzsche is voluminous. *Nietzsche's On the Genealogy of Morals: A Critical Guide* gathers many top Nietzsche scholars to discuss this work. There are also numerous attempts to synthesize all of Nietzsche's work into a single whole. Alexander Nehamas's *Nietzsche: Life as Literature* and Gilles Deleuze's *Nietzsche and Philosophy* are models of this type of scholarship.

Levinas

Levinas's two major works are *Totality and Infinity* and *Otherwise than Being*. Both works assume a great deal about the history of philosophy, as well as phenomenology as a philosophical method. He also has numerous volumes of collected essays, such as the one we read. Most of his essays deal with philosophical issues, but he also writes extensively about literature and religion.

Ethics as First Philosophy: The Significance of Emmanuel Levinas for Philosophy, Literature and Religion is a collection of essays by Levinas scholars that shows the many directions in which his thought has been taken. Adriaan Peperzak's *To the Other: An Introduction to the Philosophy of Emmanuel Levinas* offers careful readings of some of Levinas's texts. It is an excellent model of how to read Levinas.

Bibliography

Allison, Henry. *Kant's* Groundwork for the Metaphysics of Morals: A *Commentary*. Oxford: Oxford University Press, 2011.

Allison, Henry. *Kant's Theory of Freedom*. Cambridge: Cambridge University Press, 1990.

Annas, Julia. *The Morality of Happiness*. Oxford: Oxford University Press, 1995.

Aristotle. *Eudemian Ethics* in *The Complete Works of Aristotle*, 2 vols. Ed. Jonathan Barnes. Oxford: Oxford University Press, 1984.

Aristotle. *Metaphysics* in *The Complete Works of Aristotle*, 2 vols. Ed. Jonathan Barnes. Oxford: Oxford University Press, 1984.

Aristotle. *Nicomachean Ethics*. Trans. Martin Ostwald. Englewood Cliffs, NJ: Prentice Hall, 1962.

Aristotle. *On the Soul* in *The Complete Works of Aristotle*, 2 vols. Ed. Jonathan Barnes. Oxford: Oxford University Press, 1984.

Aristotle. *Politics* in *The Complete Works of Aristotle*, 2 vols. Ed. Jonathan Barnes. Oxford: Oxford University Press, 1984.

Aristotle. *Rhetoric* in *The Complete Works of Aristotle*, 2 vols. Ed. Jonathan Barnes. Oxford: Oxford University Press, 1984.

Deleuze, Gilles. *Nietzsche and Philosophy*. Trans. H. Tomlinson. New York: Columbia University Press, 1983.

Deleuze, Gilles. *Spinoza: Practical Philosophy*. Trans. Robert Hurley. San Francisco: City Lights, 1988.

Della Rocca, Michael. *Spinoza*. New York: Routledge, 2008.

Donner, Wendy and Richard Fumerton. *Mill*. Oxford: Wiley–Blackwell, 2009.

Freud, Sigmund. *The Interpretation of Dreams*. *The Standard Edition of the Complete Psychological Works of Sigmund Freud*, vol. 5. Trans. James Strachey. London: Hogarth Press, 1962.

Gensler, Harry J., Earl W. Spurgin, and James C. Swindal, eds. *Ethics: Contemporary Readings*. New York: Routledge, 2003.

The Holy Bible, *New International Version*. Colorado Springs: International Bible Society, 1984.

Israel, Jonathan. *Radical Enlightenment: Philosophy and the Making of Modernity, 1650–1750*. Oxford: Oxford University Press, 2002.

Kant, Immanuel. *Critique of the Power of Judgment*. Ed. and trans. Paul Guyer and Eric Matthews. Cambridge: Cambridge University Press, 2000.

Kant, Immanuel. *The Critique of Practical Reason* in *Practical Philosophy*. Ed. and trans. Mary J. Gregor. Cambridge: Cambridge University Press, 1996.

Kant, Immanuel. *Critique of Pure Reason*. Ed. and trans. Paul Guyer and Allen W. Wood. Cambridge: Cambridge University Press, 1998.

Kant, Immanuel. *Grounding for the Metaphysics of Morals*. Trans. James W. Ellington. Indianapolis: Hackett, 1981.

Kant, Immanuel. *The Metaphysics of Morals* in *Practical Philosophy*. Ed. and trans. Mary J. Gregor. Cambridge: Cambridge University Press, 1996.

Kant, Immanuel. "What is Enlightenment?" in *Practical Philosophy*. Ed. and trans. Mary J. Gregor. Cambridge: Cambridge University Press, 1996.

Kraut, Richard. *Aristotle on the Human Good*. Princeton: Princeton University Press, 1991.

Levinas, Emmanuel. "Ethics as First Philosophy" in *The Levinas Reader*. Trans. Seán Hand. Oxford: Blackwell, 1989.

Levinas, Emmanuel. *Otherwise than Being, Or Beyond Essence*. Trans. Alphonso Lingis. Pittsburgh: Duquesne University Press, 1998.

Levinas, Emmanuel. *Totality and Infinity*. Trans. Alphonso Lingis. Pittsburgh: Duquesne University Press, 1969.

Locke, John. *Essay Concerning Human Understanding* in *The Empiricists*. New York: Doubleday, 1961.

May, Todd. *Gilles Deleuze: An Introduction.* Cambridge: Cambridge University Press, 2005.

Mill, John Stuart. *On Liberty.* Indianapolis: Hackett, 1978.

Mill, John Stuart. *The Subjection of Women.* Mineola, NY: Dover, 1997.

Mill, John Stuart. *Utilitarianism.* Buffalo: Prometheus, 1987.

Nadler, Steven. *Spinoza's Ethics: An Introduction.* Cambridge: Cambridge University Press, 2006.

Nehamas, Alexander. *Nietzsche: Life as Literature.* Cambridge, MA: Harvard University Press, 1987.

Nietzsche, Friedrich. *Beyond Good and Evil.* Trans. Walter Kaufmann. New York: Vintage, 1989.

Nietzsche, Friedrich. *On the Genealogy of Morals.* Trans. Walter Kaufmann. New York: Vintage, 1989.

Nietzsche, Friedrich. *Thus Spoke Zarathustra.* Trans. Walter Kaufmann. New York: Penguin, 1978.

Peperzak, Adriaan, ed. *Ethics as First Philosophy: The Significance of Emmanuel Levinas for Philosophy, Literature and Religion.* New York: Routledge, 1995.

Peperzak, Adriaan. *To the Other: An Introduction to the Philosophy of Emmanuel Levinas.* West Lafayette: Purdue University Press, 2005.

Polansky, Ronald, ed. *The Cambridge Companion to Aristotle's Nicomachean Ethics.* Cambridge: Cambridge University Press, 2014.

Sartre, Jean-Paul. *The Writings of Jean-Paul Sartre, vol. 1: A Biographical Life.* Trans. Richard McCleary. Evanston: Northwestern University Press, 1974.

Skorupski, John, ed. *The Cambridge Companion to Mill.* Cambridge: Cambridge University Press, 1998.

Spinoza, Baruch. *The Essential Spinoza: Ethics and Related Writings.* Trans. Samuel Shirley. Indianapolis: Hackett, 2006.

Spinoza, Baruch. *Letters* in *Spinoza: Complete Works.* Trans. Samuel Shirley. Indianapolis: Hackett, 2002.

Spinoza, Baruch. *Short Treatise on God, Man, and his Well-Being* in *Spinoza: Complete Works.* Trans. Samuel Shirley. Indianapolis: Hackett, 2002.

Spinoza, Baruch. *Spinoza: Complete Works.* Trans. Samuel Shirley. Indianapolis: Hackett, 2002.

Spinoza, Baruch. *Theological–Political Treatise* in *Spinoza: Complete Works.* Trans. Samuel Shirley. Indianapolis: Hackett, 2002.

Spinoza, Baruch. *The Treatise on the Emendation of the Intellect* in *Spinoza: Complete Works.* Trans. Samuel Shirley. Indianapolis: Hackett, 2002.

Wood, Allen. *Kantian Ethics.* Cambridge: Cambridge University Press, 2007.

Index